ENDORS

I've known Asher Intrater for more than thirty years. He is a man of great integrity and a leading voice in the Messianic Jewish community. He has helped many Christians grow in their understanding of God's plan to restore His creation through fulfilling His covenants with the Jewish people for the benefit of the nations. In *Alignment*, Asher skillfully connects prophecies and promises in Scripture to illustrate what God is doing in our lifetime. I know you will be blessed by the revelations in this book!

ROBERT MORRIS, SENIOR PASTOR, GATEWAY CHURCH
BESTSELLING AUTHOR OF *THE BLESSED LIFE*,
BEYOND BLESSED, AND *TAKE THE DAY OFF*

I first discovered the work of Asher Intrater when I read his book *Who Ate Lunch With Abraham?* I was profoundly impacted by the appearances of Jesus in Old Testament passages that I had known and studied my whole life but had never seen properly. In this new book, *Alignment*, he beautifully threads together the events of Scripture to articulate God's immense love for us. This book is sure to ignite your passion for Jerusalem and the greatest story ever told. In such a divisive time, this work illustrates what God can and will do through the unity of believers.

JOSH MORRIS, FOUNDER AND CEO, TOV CO.

In Asher's book, *Alignment*, he describes the wholeness of Scripture, God's heart for the believer, Israel, and the nations. He paints a great picture of what it means to be in sync with the Person of Yeshua. When we align our heart with His, we assign the same value that God assigns to souls, family, communities, and the world. As Asher states, "God's alignment represents His authority on earth: His King, Jesus; His capital, Jerusalem."

JONATHAN WEISS, ISRAEL LIAISON,
DAYSTAR TELEVISION NETWORK

This powerful, prophetic teaching is a must for the churches all over the world and the Messianic Jews to fulfill their prophetic destiny together. It is clear, pointed, easy to understand, and will often lead to the response "Of course! How did I not see that before?"

DANIEL C. JUSTER, THD, RESTORATION FROM ZION

As the Spirit of God continues to entrust him with depths of wisdom and revelation, Asher faithfully walks out these truths in humble and costly obedience to the Lord through his personal life and through ministry. I deeply appreciate how this Jewish father has opened up the hearts of our Arab family in a way I have not witnessed before. This book infuses hope in all of us as our heavenly Father draws His global family together into full alignment and kingdom restoration that we may be one as He and His Son are one.

DAVID DEMIAN, WATCHMEN FOR THE NATIONS

Alignment is a word God has been highlighting in this season in the body of Christ. In this book, Asher scripturally defines the most critical aspect of alignment as being between Israel and the international church, or ecclesia. The link joining the two is the Messianic Jewish remnant. As we move close to the Lord's return, there is coming a revelation of the necessity of alignment with the root from which we have been taken (Romans 11:16–18).

JANE HANSEN HOYT, AGLOW INTERNATIONAL

I recommend the ministry of Asher Intrater. Personally, he is one of my favorite Bible teachers. He has an unusual depth of insight into God's Word with clarity into the Lord's prophetic purposes that are unfolding in the earth in this generation.

MIKE BICKLE, FOUNDER,
INTERNATIONAL HOUSE OF PRAYER KANSAS CITY
ASHER CHEERLEADER

Some of Asher's books are standard reading material in many Bible schools of the nations. This writing, I believe, will join the others as he speaks to the subject of alignment. This work, like all the rest, was born out of decades of prayer and study, and I know you will glean revelation and deep wisdom from these pages.

PAUL WILBUR, INTERNATIONAL WORSHIP ARTIST,
WILBUR MINISTRIES

I love the message of this book! Coming into true heart agreement—with God and with each other—brings the kingdom of heaven to earth.

EITAN SHISHKOFF, FOUNDER,
TENTS OF MERCY AND FIELDS OF WHEAT

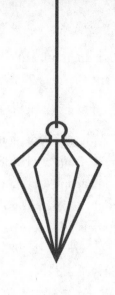

ALIGNMENT

ASHER INTRATER

CHARISMA
HOUSE

ALIGNMENT by Asher Intrater
Published by Charisma House, an imprint of Charisma Media
600 Rinehart Road, Lake Mary, Florida 32746

Cover design and interior layout by Diego Polly

While the author has made every effort to provide accurate internet addresses at the time of publication, neither the publisher nor the author assumes any responsibility for errors or for changes that occur after publication. Further, the publisher does not have any control over and does not assume any responsibility for author or third-party websites or their content.

For more Spirit-led resources, visit charismamedia.com and the author's website at tikkunglobal.org.

Cataloging-in-Publication Data is on file with the Library of Congress.
International Standard Book Number: 978-1-63641-349-5
E-book ISBN: 978-1-63641-350-1

23 24 25 26 27 — 9 8 7 6 5 4 3 2 1
Printed in the United States of America

Most Charisma Media products are available at special quantity discounts for bulk purchase for sales promotions, premiums, fund-raising, and educational needs. For details, call us at (407) 333-0600 or visit our website at www.charismamedia.com.

TABLE OF CONTENTS

Section Two: The Abrahamic Family

Section Three: Restoration of All Things

Section Four: The Glorification of Jerusalem

Section Five: Synergy

Afterword

Appendix 252

Thanks 256

Foreword

by Francis Chan

Before reading this book, I rarely prayed for Israel. I am embarrassed to admit that I have gone months, maybe even years, without thinking about this nation. It wasn't until I understood God's feelings and plan for Israel that my heart changed. Hopefully this book will open your eyes in the same way.

Like many American Christians, I spent a fair amount of time trying to discern God's will for my life, but rarely thought about His will for this earth. What I didn't realize is that I couldn't fully know His will for me without understanding His plans for Israel and the earth. It's like I have been building a carburetor my whole life without realizing that it was part of a car.

I recently participated in a Bible study with Asher and several other Messianic Jews in Jerusalem. It didn't take long for me to discover that they study the Scriptures differently than I do. I was taught to read a passage and ask: "What do I think it says?" and "How does it apply to my life?" They focused less on self, instead asking: "How does this fit with everything else God says?" and "What does this reveal about His plan for heaven and earth?"

I have studied and taught the Bible for over forty years. I went to Bible college and seminary, and I have devoted myself to knowing the Scriptures. My mind has been full of countless pieces of biblical information, but it wasn't until I read some of Asher's writings that I saw how those pieces came together beautifully into the cohesive story of God.

Do you remember doing "dot to dot" puzzles as a child? We saw a page of seemingly random dots and numbers, and when we took a pencil and traced the dots together—magic! A picture appeared that made sense of all of the dots. This is what *Alignment* will do for many of us.

For those who grew up studying the Bible, most of the facts in this book will not surprise you. These are truths we have believed and loved for years. What may shock you is just how beautifully these truths have woven together over the past six thousand years. *Alignment* will bring to light passages that you have read but maybe never understood. What has happened and is happening in Israel will finally make sense to you and excite you.

The Bible has never been more beautiful and glorious to me. I have never loved the Word more, nor have I ever been more convinced that the Bible contains the very words of God. I pray that the same awe and love is awakened in you as you read this book.

Francis Chan
Director, Crazy Love Ministries

Preface

to the Second Edition

The first publication of *Alignment* in 2017 brought about some explosive reactions. Most of them were quite positive. But some of them were negative.

Particularly a group of conservative evangelical pastors in Israel took a stance in opposition to the book, which created a serious conflict in the local Messianic community here for quite a few years.

At first I couldn't understand at all what they were criticizing. However, since many of them were honest brothers in the Lord, I decided to try my best to listen to their concerns. This led to a set of dialogues that took hundreds of hours.

Some of the objections had to do with differences in theology, others with differences in terminology. Some were accusations of character faults.

The time was extremely painful. We did everything we could to repent of pride. This led to us repenting before the national evangelical elders' assembly several times.

It also led to deep line-by-line discussions about biblical texts.

I began to see how people from a more conservative theological background could take offense at what we had said. And we began to see how many aspects of the "charismatic" world are seen as hype and exaggeration. This led to a group of us writing a declaration of repentance concerning the charismatic body as a whole that was signed by many leaders around the world. The main body of that statement can be seen in the appendix.

After some four years of debate and division, the whole issue was finally brought to a vote at the Israeli evangelical elders' assembly. By the grace of God, the great majority came to a decision that we had been through enough conflict on the issue, and we could vote not to continue a judicial process. This seemed to me to be a significant breakthrough for unity and understanding.

The vote was clearly not "in favor" of us, but in favor of accepting one another with different perspectives. There has been a beautiful spirit of unity and harmony in the body since then.

This season has been quite humbling for me. And coming out of a painful situation with more humility is always a good thing.

We agreed to take the book off the market until we could make changes. I have made approximately one hundred changes in the text. And we have kept the book off the market for well over a year. Now it is time to release the edited version.

If we want to be people of honesty before the Lord, we have to be willing to listen patiently to those who are criticizing us, no matter how painful the process.

I had to struggle with feelings that I had been betrayed by some of these conservative leaders. But in prayer I felt the Lord told me that I am responsible for whatever happens from my skin inwards. What other people do is their responsibility. I have to take responsibility for my own thoughts, actions, and attitudes.

To me the great victory is that during the whole process I kept loving and praying for these brothers. Victory is not winning an argument but loving those who oppose you—and loving them while they are opposing you. In looking back, I am happy that it all happened, and that God worked the situation for good.

Since the writing of this book in 2017, many cataclysmic events have taken place around the world, including the coronavirus, political upheavals, natural disasters, and even the Russia-Ukraine war. I have not addressed those here, as that was not the purpose of this book. This is primarily a re-edit of the original text in the light of a wider perspective.

May you receive this new edition in the grace and humility in which it is intended.

In Yeshua's love,

Asher

Remnant and Ecclesia

For the past few years, three topics have been exploding in my heart and also seem to have burdened the hearts of dear friends around the world:

1. Global Alignment
2. The Abrahamic Family
3. Restoration of All Things.

"Global Alignment" has to do with right relationships for true Christians around the world and for the Messianic remnant of Israel in order to be ready for the second coming of Yeshua (Jesus). Alignment is submitting to God's order and prepares us for establishing His kingdom on earth.

"The Abrahamic Family" has to do with understanding our relationship as believers in Yeshua as a family, not only in heaven but also on earth. God is our Father; we are His children; a Father wants His family united. Our identity as a family goes back to Abraham's family, and our search for unity must go all the way back to that "first" family.

The Abrahamic family includes the Jewish people, the whole church and reconciliation between Arabs and Jews through faith in Yeshua.

"Restoration of All Things" has to do with our belief that despite intense persecution and tribulation in the end times, there will also be a widespread revival leading up to the second coming. That revival will lead to a spiritual restoration of all the good things God has promised within the hearts of the people of God **before the return of Yeshua.** And then **after the return of Yeshua**, that restoration will be manifested outwardly into a perfected world society with perfected people as its citizens.

Global alignment is about being in right order for the kingdom of God.

Abraham's family is about being in right relationship as the family of God.

Restoration is about believing for all good things in God's plan to come to pass.

A fourth section is about "The Glorification of the City of Jerusalem." According to Isaiah 60, there will be a manifestation of the glory of God in the city of Jerusalem, partially during the period of the tribulation before the second coming, and then more fully after the second coming.

How does the promise of a manifestation of God's glory in Zion impact the international church ecclesia and the nation of Israel? Who is involved and what will happen? I have tried to "unpack" just a little bit of that prophecy toward the end of the book.

And finally, there is a small but very important fifth section about "Synergy." Divine alignment leads up to a divine synergy. When we put the pieces together, a much greater result is produced than just the sum of the individual parts. It is an explosive release of spiritual power for the kingdom of God.

This book is designed to help us understand these biblical concepts. In some ways, these topics represent a Messianic ecclesiology—a Jewish way of understanding the international Christian church in its highest and most positive sense of the word. A progressive understanding is being revealed to us all in these days about who we are as the global community of faith.

My intention is that this will not be just a teaching *about* these ideas but provide a practical manual and an architectural design to help bring them to pass—both impartation and implementation. It is to mobilize us into that right alignment, to bring us together as a family, and to prepare us for revival in the end times.

I hope the book will encourage and strengthen your faith.

May you be "synergized" by it!

1

ALIGNMENT

*Yeshua's submission to the heavenly Father
and the divine glory in Him from the Father
comprise the perfect alignment from which
all other alignment flows.*

1

May They All Be One!

This is why you need to have a cooperative heart: Everything starts with God's heart as a Father and His love for us. He wanted to create a family with real children made in His image (Genesis 1:26). There had to be a divine pattern for human beings in the image of God. That image of God and man together is found in the "Anointed One"—the Christos. This is Yeshua (Jesus)—the Messiah.

The amazing love of God desires not only that we worship Him as His creatures, but also that we join together with Him as a family (Ephesians 3:14–15), that we become partakers of His divine nature (II Peter 1:4), and that we become one with Him (John 17:21–23).

> *The sacrifice of Yeshua on the cross*
> *makes the divine alignment possible for us.*
> *Yeshua's death and resurrection is the*
> *magnet that pulls us into that divine unity.*

God made us physically from the same material found in the earth around us, but then He blew His Spirit into us (Genesis 2:7). We have a paradoxical nature; we have two essential parts that do not seem to fit together so easily. We are part dirt and part the Spirit of God. Yeshua is the answer to that paradox. He is both God and man. Yeshua brings God's will down into the earth and raises mankind up to our destiny. He is the pattern of everything God wants for us. He is the center of God's plan.

At one of the highest moments of revelation in the Scriptures, Yeshua prays for us to fulfill that destiny. He prays for us to be one with our heavenly Father, even as He is.

Yeshua brings God's will down into the earth and raises mankind up to our destiny.

May they all be one, even as you Father are in Me and I in You, may they also be in Us, in order that the world may believe that You have sent Me. I have given them the glory which You have given Me, in order that they will be one even as We are one. I in them and You in Me so that they will be made perfect by being one, in order that the world may know that You have sent Me and that You love them as You love Me.

—John 17:21–23

What amazing promises there are in this prayer! Yeshua prays that we will become one with God; that we will have divine glory; that we will be made perfect; that we will experience God's love just as Yeshua does. Union with God, divine glory, spiritual perfection, intimacy with our heavenly Father—all in one prayer. This prayer is the pinnacle of God's will for us.

Everything good that will happen to us occurs "as it is" with Yeshua and the Father. We enter into a pattern, an order and relationship that already exist. This divine love and glory have existed **"since before the foundation of the world" (verse 24).**

When we talk about "alignment," we need to realize that the alignment started here. The alignment already exists. Yeshua is aligned with our heavenly Father. We are not inventing an alignment; we are entering into an alignment that is predetermined. All our alignment is based on the pattern of "as it is" with Yeshua. He is the Son in perfect alignment with the Father. Everything else just "falls in line."

Although Yeshua and the Father are one, Yeshua is submitted to the Father. There is an alignment of authority, honor, precedence, and will. Yeshua said, **"The Father is greater than I" (John 14:28)**, and I do **"nothing unless the Father shows Me" (John 5:19)**. Yeshua prayed,

"Not My will be done but Yours" (Matthew 26:39).

At the same time, the Father has given all authority to Yeshua; anyone who wants to honor the Father must honor the Son (John 5:23); they are one (John 10:30); the only way to come to the Father is through the Son (John 14:6). Yeshua's submission to the heavenly Father and the divine glory in Him from the Father comprise the perfect alignment from which all other alignment flows.

This alignment is a pathway that has been prepared beforehand for us to walk in (Ephesians 2:10). We are drawn into that pathway by God's love and grace. The sacrifice of Yeshua on the cross makes the divine alignment possible for us. Yeshua's death and resurrection is the magnet that pulls us into that divine unity.

God is Father. A father is a combination of love and authority. Love without authority is a friend, not a father. Authority without love is a boss, not a father. Since God our Father is both love and authority, we are drawn into alignment with Him. That alignment has both intimacy and submission. There is intimacy because of His love; there is submission because of His authority.

When we have a tender heart and a sensitive conscience, we look for this alignment of intimacy and submission in every situation. In any group or organization, most people seek only what is good for themselves. That self-centered attitude limits and frustrates what could come out of the group if there were more cooperation and unity. A greater good can always be achieved.

Alignment is an order that allows for everyone to have his or her own place—for everyone to function, for everyone to bear fruit. Alignment is an order based on intimacy and submission. It starts with Yeshua and the Father and extends into every possible group when two or more people are gathered together for a common purpose. For the sake of the greater good of the group, one must be willing to submit to the authority of that group.

If a violinist joins a symphony orchestra, he wants to produce the best music. He does not join for the sake of the order of the orchestra but for the beautiful music. On the other hand, if there is not order, there will be no music at all, only noise. The violinist will want to submit to the leading of the conductor of the orchestra. He will want everyone to submit to that order. He will want the cellist and the pianist and the percussionist to be aligned with the conductor so that there can be beautiful music. If there is no alignment with the conductor, there will be no symphony.

["Phon" here means "sound," as in *phonics*. "Sym" means "together with," as in s*ympathy*. A symphony is sounds flowing together. The beauty is in the harmony. Alignment produces harmony which makes for the beauty. (We'll deal with "synergy" and "synthesis" in chapter 25.)]

The same principle holds true for any group. A sports team needs to be aligned with the coach's plan. A successful business needs to be aligned with the boss, a church with its pastor, a family with the dad, a government with its prime minister, an army with its commander. How much more so when we talk about God's plan for mankind and for His creation!

The reason there are assigned and numbered seats at a ball game, airplane, or theater is to make sure that everyone has a place. The order is to protect the weak. Without it, every bully would push the weaker people out of the way. God's plan has order because He wants everyone to have a place.

A good-hearted person will seek the greater good. The greater good demands cooperation. Cooperation needs alignment and submission with the plans of the leader. **A good-hearted person will seek to be aligned with the purposes of the group and its leadership.**

Whenever we come into a group, we look to cooperate for the common goal. We immediately seek to understand what that goal is and who is in leadership. We submit both to the authority and the purpose. We are team players with a cooperative attitude.

In Israel, we have a dozen political parties for a country of 9.5 million people. I try to imagine what it would be like to be the prime minister. How does he even get out of bed in the morning? How can he face such difficulties? What would it be like to see things from his point of view? One prime minister, who used to be in the opposition party, said when he took office, "It looks different from here than it did from there."

If there were an Olympic competition for complaining and arguing, no doubt we in Israel would win the gold. In an embarrassing way, it is part of our culture and identity that no one wants to cooperate with anyone. A cooperative, submissive attitude is seen as weakness. The attitude is: "Only weak people cooperate and submit." How tragic and how frustrating!

Spiritual strength and self-discipline are needed to see someone else's perspective. Anyone can see his own perspective. That is natural. Extra spiritual effort to rise above one's own instincts is needed to see someone else's.

I often use the example of shekel and *shemesh*. Shekel is the Israeli coin; *shemesh* is the word for "sun." If you hold up a coin to your eye, it appears to be the same size as the sun. Yeshua said to take the beam out of our own eye before we take the speck out of the eye of another (Matthew 7:1–3).

It is human tendency to see what we do right as enormously important, and what someone else does right as insignificant. And likewise, we have the tendency to see whatever we do wrong as microscopically small, and whatever someone else does wrong as enormously reprehensible.

To come into right alignment, we have to deflate our own self-importance and inflate the importance of someone else's perspective. It is a worthy spiritual exercise to hear and understand another person's heart.

When we want to be aligned with God's plan, we have to pray again and again, as Yeshua did in Gethsemane, **"Not my will but Yours be done" (Matthew 26:39)**. We change our will to be aligned with His. We are to seek the right order that God has set up. We seek first the kingdom of God and His righteousness, and then the other things will fall into place (Matthew 6:33).

Since God's order includes everyone and everything, we have to learn to respect other people, their gifts, their purposes, and their history. We respect the precedence of what has happened before us. We respect history and honor people. That helps to bring us into alignment with God's purposes.

It is a worthy spiritual exercise to hear and understand another person's heart.

We see an example of that in Yeshua's baptism in water by John. Yeshua was greater than John, and Yeshua had not sinned. So why did He need to be immersed in water? One reason is that in the first century, baptism in water meant not only repentance of sin, but dedication to holiness, cleansing from the influences of the world, and submission to the spiritual leader at the time.

Yeshua said He would be baptized by John in **"order to fulfill all righteousness" (Matthew 3:15)**. He submitted to God's right order. What a beautiful example of righteousness we see at Yeshua's baptism! John was the anointed prophet of his generation. Yeshua submitted to him, just as He submitted to Miriam (Mary) and Joseph as His parents (Luke 2:51).

Yeshua submitted to someone lesser than Himself to be aligned to God's plan and order. Being baptized by John was part of that alignment. When the other religious leaders refused to submit to John through baptism, they rejected that alignment, that righteous order (Luke 7:29) and, in fact, showed themselves to be unworthy of God's plan for their own lives (Luke 7:30).

Yeshua submitted first to His heavenly Father, then to His earthly parents, and then to John the Baptist as a prophet. He set Himself in right order and right alignment with God's purposes for His own life. Let us follow in His footsteps as we seek to align ourselves with God's purposes as well.

Questions for Reflection

1. How does Yeshua fulfill the statement in Genesis 1:26 that God made man in His image?

2. What does it mean to be "one" with God according to John 17?

3. How does God love us as a Father?

4. How do we "fall in line" with the relationship between God and Yeshua?

5. Why should we have a cooperative and submissive attitude?

2

Natural and Moral Law

Most people think they are right and everyone else is wrong. We could summarize almost all arguments in history as one person saying, "I'm right and you're wrong," while the other says, "No, I'm right and you're wrong." The biblical viewpoint is that God created us good, but we have all sinned (Genesis 3, 6; I Kings 8:46; Psalm 14, 53; Ecclesiastes 7:20; Isaiah 53:6; Romans 3:23).

I suppose we could say with a bit of dry humor that God enters the argument and says, "No, you're both wrong. I'm right."

> *Accepting God's standards both physically and morally is part of being rightly aligned with our Creator. He made us and we belong to Him (Psalm 100:3).*

The beginning of the message of the biblical prophets was that we all have to admit that we are wrong, and that God is right. **"For in the gospel the righteousness of God is revealed" (Romans 1:16–17).** It does not do any good to skip over God's righteousness and try to establish our own righteousness. **"For by trying to establish their own righteousness, they have not submitted to the righteousness of God" (Romans 10:3).**

This is how we start the process of alignment in our own lives.

1. We recognize that we are "out of line."
2. We recognize that God has the right alignment.
3. We change our position.
4. We get in line with His alignment.

The Bible calls this "repentance." It is a moral change. It is a change of will. There is no way to get into right alignment without this change, without repenting.

It seems to me that there are two kinds of repentance. There is the "big" repentance, which happens usually once in a lifetime when we turn away from the things of the world and choose to believe in God and follow His Messiah. (This may happen more than once in the case of serious backsliding or falling away.)

Then there is the second kind of repentance: this repentance is a daily turning away from the "world, the flesh and the devil," which are around us all the time. In this second type, we repent every day and forgive those who have sinned against us (Matthew 6:12). Then we walk forward with the Lord in faith.

This kind of daily repentance/realignment is like following a compass on a hiking trail or a GPS navigating program like Waze. You continually check the compass and adjust your path to follow the coordinates. We keep changing in order to "stay in line" as we move forward. Our alignment with the Lord is a living and dynamic relationship. We have to keep changing, keep repenting, and keep moving forward. Yeshua is walking; we follow after Him.

Repentance is the first step of alignment; the second step is faith. If we believe in God, we believe in the One He has sent, the chosen Messiah. Yeshua (Jesus) is that Messiah. In every generation, the Israelites had to believe and submit to the chosen prophet or king (Exodus 14:31). That was part of the faith. Yeshua is the chosen anointed One over all the generations (John 14:1).

To believe in Yeshua is to submit to Him. The declaration of salvation is **"Yeshua is Lord" (Romans 10:9).** What does it mean to say that Yeshua is Lord? It is a verbal commitment to do whatever He says. Yeshua said, **"Why do you call me Lord, Lord, and don't do what I say?" (Luke 6:46).**

To call Yeshua "Lord" is to make a commitment to **obedience**. To be

| *Our alignment with the Lord is a living and dynamic relationship. We have to keep changing, keep repenting, and keep moving forward.* |

saved is to do what He says. If someone says that Yeshua is Lord but does not do what He says, then he may be just deceiving himself (Matthew 7:21–23; Romans 1:5, 6:16, 16:26; I John 1:6, 2:4).

We believe and receive what Yeshua freely gave us on the cross. Because of that, we submit to Him as Lord and commit to do whatever He tells us. This process of alignment with God starts with these three steps:

1. Repent and forgive.

2. Believe and receive.

3. Commit and submit.

After that there is a lifetime "walk of faith." We receive the Holy Spirit (Luke 11:13; Acts 2:38), power (Acts 1:8), tongues and prophecy (Acts 2:2–4; 2:17–18; 10:44–46; 19:6), fruit of the Spirit (Galatians 5:22), gifts of the Spirit (I Corinthians 12, 14), the fellowship of His sufferings (II Corinthians 1:3–9, Philippians 3:10, I Peter 4), sanctification (II Corinthians 7:1; Hebrews 12:10), and at the end, glorification (Romans 8:39, I Corinthians 2:7).

The writings of the apostles describe this process in detail, and it is not the purpose of this book to teach on those topics. However, because there is so much emphasis today on God's wonderful promises for personal blessings, I wanted to note that we cannot "skip over" or ignore these basic stages of repentance and obedience in the process. The Lordship of Yeshua is the cornerstone of our personal alignment with God's plans and purposes.

Alignment brings us into a God-given **set of priorities** for our personal lives. In the Gospels, Yeshua outlined some of those simple priorities. Eternal life is the most important: **"What does it profit a man to gain the**

whole world and lose his soul?" (Matthew 16:26). He also taught that the soul is more important than the body, and the body is more important than clothes (Matthew 6:25).

Although it is much more complex than this, we could try to summarize the order of priority for our personal lives as:

1. Spirit
2. Soul
3. Body
4. Family
5. Finances.

Part of alignment is to accept ourselves as created beings and God as our Creator. He created all things; therefore, He knows how they work. If you put wrong desires in your spirit, your spirit will be weak and sick (Mark 4:24, I Corinthians 11:30). If you put wrong food in your body, your body will be weak and sick.

Since God created the whole material world and all that is in it, He has no difficulty in supplying our personal needs and provisions. However, we have to "play by the rules." [And worrying about the situation does not help in any case (Matthew 6:25).]

We submit to God's **created order** and His **moral standards**. Part of the human spirit is the conscience. The conscience is designed to be an internal guide to the moral standards of God (Romans 2:15). Unfortunately, our consciences have been warped by years of sin, lust, guilt, rebellion, and lies. We have to clean and recalibrate our consciences so that we can hear from God correctly. **Spiritual alignment is moral alignment.**

We recalibrate our conscience by meditation on Scriptures, repentance and forgiveness, righteous actions, Spirit-led prayer, and by faith in Yeshua's atoning sacrifice. These steps will help clean our consciences from sin and guilt (Hebrews 4:12; 9:9, 14; 10:22).

Guilt to the human conscience is like pain to the human body. The conscience will do anything to remove guilt. The correct way is what is described above (and constitutes the main theme of the Book of Hebrews).

The Lordship of Yeshua is the cornerstone of our personal alignment with God's plans and purposes.

However, if a person does not have the ability to cleanse his conscience by the blood of the Lamb, then his conscience will begin to readjust its own calibration.

This recalibration will be done either by increasing the condemnation of others (what I did wrong isn't so bad; look what that other person did), or by lowering moral standards to dismiss the claim of wrongdoing (I'm only human and not to blame, and everyone does this anyway).

Many people try to perceive what God is saying by their own feelings. However, emotions are much less tuned to the Holy Spirit than the conscience. **The conscience is a central part of the heart and tells us what is right and wrong.** The conscience is the *green light, yellow light, red light* warning system on the inside.

(The words *heart* and *conscience* are used interchangeably in such passages as I Samuel 24:5; Jeremiah 31:33; Romans 2:15; II Corinthians 5:11; I Timothy 1:5; Hebrews 10:22; and I John 3:20–21.)

God's Spirit bears witness with our human spirit (Romans 8:16). The conscience is the part of our spirit which perceives the voice of God. The way we hear God is by God's Spirit communicating to our inward conscience. **"My conscience is bearing witness with me in the Holy Spirit" (Romans 9:1).**

It is the lack of moral discernment which makes many of us "charismatics" seem flaky. The Holy Spirit is more "moral" than "mystical." We should desire holiness not spiritism. When someone prophesies in a mystical way, but there is no moral clarity to the words, something is wrong. I do not want to hear "gooey" prophecies. We should hunger and thirst for righteousness.

The Holy Spirit's leading is more "ethical" than "emotional." The misunderstanding that the "heart" is more your emotions than your conscience has led many astray (I Timothy 1:19). What you feel emotionally is not always what God is trying to tell you. There is purity to the prophetic word of God. It is a feeling that is more conscience-based than emotion-based.

God is more interested in our being "conformed" to the image of Yeshua than He is in our being "comfortable" in our circumstances. Prophecy does give us comfort (I Corinthians 14:3), but the spirit of comfort does not mean being comfortable.

Biblical comfort is an inward power to enable you to stand in the midst of suffering and persecution. We have spiritual encouragement (comfort) to strengthen us in the midst of trials in order to encourage others (II Corinthians 1:4). We have the "comfort of Christ" to the same degree we stand in the **"sufferings of Christ" (verse 5).**

Let us restore the moral "cutting edge" to the prophetic gifts. Moral correction is a significant part of God's realignment for us in these end times. How can we be aligned if we cannot receive correction (Proverbs 15:31–33)?

Moral correction is also part of the healing process. We believe in divine healing. By the wounds of Yeshua we have been healed (Matthew 8:17). Healing is in the atonement just as much as forgiveness of sins. Salvation includes both forgiveness and healing. Yeshua gave us authority to heal the sick (Matthew 10:1).

There is also divine healing in the bread and wine of communion, if we take the elements with full faith. Yeshua gave His body and soul to heal and save our body and soul.

Part of communion is that we **"examine" ourselves** (I Corinthians 11:28). There may be something wrong spiritually inside of us that is preventing us from being healed. **"It is for this reason that many of you are weak and sick" (verse 30).** If we examine ourselves and remove what is wrong, then we can be healed. If we don't examine ourselves and remove what is wrong, then we will remain sick. Self-examination during communion can bring healing. That examination is part of alignment.

Remember the priorities Yeshua taught us. The spirit and the soul are more important than the body. If we get realigned with God's will, then there will be nothing to prevent our healing. It would be better to lose an arm or leg or eye altogether than to have sin in our heart and be in danger of punishment (Matthew 5:28–30).

Not all healing is supernatural. God also gives us directions to eat healthy, live actively, keep clean, separate things that cause infection, get enough rest, and so on. God made nature and the *laws of nature*.

Since God made natural creation, anything that is patently unnatural is not of God. While there is no direct commandment against cigarette smoking, it is obvious that taking smoke into the delicate pink tissues of lungs can only do damage. Cigarettes cause cancer; drugs destroy brain cells; junk food fouls up the digestive system.

Alignment also has to do with sexual values. God created sex. He created man and woman. He commanded us to be faithful in marriage. Sexual pleasure within the context of marital fidelity and intimacy is an amazing expression of the grace of God. But God made the rules:

1. Man and woman.

2. Marriage covenant.

3. Mutual respect (I Thessalonians 4:3–7).

It is not too hard to understand.

No matter what modern psychology and entertainment tell us, adultery is against God's moral law. Adultery is sin. Pornography is destructive. To flood ourselves with audio-visual images of lust will overload our emotional and hormonal capacity to function. God created us physically in a way to enjoy sexual pleasure, and He gave us moral laws to protect our marital relationships.

In the onslaught of propaganda promoting homosexuality and lesbianism as a gender alternative, we need to remember the simple facts of biology. There is nothing more unnatural than same-sex intercourse. It is a physical contradiction. To do something so contrary to the anatomy of the human body has no recourse but to cause devastating physical and psychological damage.

Every cell of a man's body has an X and Y chromosome; every cell of a woman's is XX. A so-called "sex change operation" would have to change every cell of the body. Even to an atheist, obvious biological facts should be enough to show what is right and wrong.

The slogan "I was born this way" is used as propaganda to promote homosexuality and lesbianism. The biological facts are just the opposite. One is born a boy or a girl. That's the way you were born. You can call your dog a cat and your cat a dog, but in the end they are still a dog and a cat.

One can argue about theology and morality endlessly. When there are foundational differences of opinion on theology or morality, one has to return to basic natural law. Physical "facts of nature" should form a common ground of objectivity for those who disagree on spiritual issues.

Paul called homosexuality and lesbianism fundamentally "unnatural" (Romans 1:26–27). To indoctrinate a younger generation to condone actions so unnatural and so psychologically damaging is cruel.

Accepting God's standards both physically and morally is part of being rightly aligned with our Creator. He made us, and we belong to Him (Psalm 100:3). He is a loving Father who is all-powerful and totally pure.

Questions for Reflection

1. Do we have to obey God in order to be saved?
2. What is the role of the conscience?
3. Is modern charismatic prophecy missing an element of holiness?
4. Is there a connection between moral laws and natural creation?

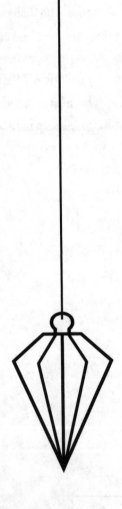

3

Historical Background of the Original Apostolic Community

As we are aligned with the love of God and His moral and natural law, so are we aligned to one another as the community of people who believe in God.

In the Gospels, we find Yeshua traveling, teaching, and healing the sick. People began to gather around Him. Multitudes came to His public meetings, and a large core group of people traveled around with Him regularly.

> *As we are aligned with the love of God and His moral and natural law, so are we aligned to one another as the community of people who believe in God.*

There were very few non-Jews among those people. He told His disciples to teach only to Jews (Matthew 10:6). When He healed or even spoke to a non-Jew, the situation was considered quite unusual (e.g., Canaanite woman, Matthew 15; Roman centurion, Luke 7; Samaritan woman, John 4).

Let's look at the historical background for a moment.

Hebrew Bible: The Hebrew Bible (Tanakh, Old Testament) came into its final form and compilation early in the fourth century BC. (I estimate that date because there are some seven to nine generations after the Babylonian exile listed in the genealogies of I Chronicles.)

Greek conquest: In 332 BC, the entire Middle East was conquered by the Greeks. Greek culture, philosophy, and language highly influenced the civilized world at that time, for better or for worse, including the Jewish community in Israel.

Greek Bible: Around 200 BC the Hebrew Bible was translated into Greek by seventy Greek and Rabbinic scholars. This translation is known as the Septuagint. Care and research were invested in this edition. Since the Hebrew versions at this time were scattered, handwritten copies, the Septuagint soon gained popularity and a certain textual authority both in the Jewish and Greek societies. It was the only "authorized" version, so to speak. Many of the quotes in the later Greek manuscripts of the New Covenant (New Testament) referencing the Hebrew Scriptures were citations from the Septuagint version.

Maccabean revolt: In 167 BC, the Jewish Maccabean revolt took over the country, established a Jewish state, and reformed the Temple worship. The different Jewish streams of faith and religion, such as the Sadducees, Pharisees, and Essenes, came out of this period.

Roman conquest: In 63 BC, the Romans under General Pompeii conquered the Middle East. Israel became a Roman protectorate. The period of Yeshua and His disciples took place under Roman rule. The Jewish people suffered at this time from religious corruption at the hands of the Sadducees and the Pharisees, as well as political corruption at the hands of Roman rulers (such as Pilate and Herod).

Messianic expectations: At the same time, expectations of the coming Messiah were intense. All of the people, from religious cults to the common working class, had expectations of some sort of Messianic kingdom that would manifest. There were different groups with different interpretations of what that kingdom would look like. This is the climate of the first century AD into which Yeshua was born.

All of Yeshua's followers were Hebrew-speaking (and Aramaic), native born, Israeli Jews. The majority were from the Galilee. They were not religious fanatics or professional clergy, as many were in the Jerusalem area. They were mostly working-class people. They were easily identifiable by the Jerusalemites for their simple lifestyle and for their Galilean accent when speaking Hebrew (Matthew 26:69, 73).

The people following Yeshua became a popular, "grassroots" movement, with obvious Messianic expectations. In the view of the New Covenant, this group represented the community of people who were following the true Messiah. They were the true remnant. They were like the company of people following David after he was anointed to be king but while he was still persecuted by King Saul.

This group was carrying the prophetic destiny of the kingdom which was promised to David and his descendants. From the viewpoint of the Gospels, this group was the "cherry" or the "cream of the crop" of the history of the Jewish people. They carried the hope of the Messianic kingdom in the midst of religious and political corruption. They were the chosen of the chosen, the remnant of the remnant.

This is the formative root of what became the apostolic community in the Book of Acts. This Messianic community was the end result of a long historical process which began with Abraham, then Moses, then David, and then the prophets. This development occurred in several major periods. Here is a simplified explanation of that historical development:

1. **Covenant Family of Abraham**—Abraham was the first believer to start the covenant community with God. Since there was no one else at the time, the covenant community was primarily his children and the employees in his household. But God made a covenant with them that they would grow to be like the stars of heaven (Genesis 15:5; 17:2).

2. **Priestly People under Moses**—This family became the large group of people who separated from Egypt at the time of Moses. The number at the Exodus was probably around three million people. It was comprised of Israelites and a mixed multitude from other nations (Exodus 12:38). They received the moral law, the priestly rituals, and the destiny to be a chosen people. There had been no identifiable "people" group connected with God until this point.

3. **Israelite Kingdom under David**—Their descendants eventually

conquered the land of Israel and set up the kingdom-state under David. The vision developed from a holy priestly people in the wilderness to the Davidic kingdom in the land of Israel. Unfortunately, that kingdom dynasty was plagued by sin and corruption.

4. **Messianic Vision of the Prophets**—After years of seeing the weaknesses of the Davidic dynasty, the prophets, starting with Isaiah, began to envision a "better" kingdom. It would be David's kingdom but improved. There would be a special king, who would be pure and righteous. His kingdom would be peaceful and prosperous. All the promises of God would be fulfilled in it. This was the Messianic hope of the prophets.

5. **Galilean Followers of Yeshua**—That prophetic vision prepared the way for Yeshua's message and mission. Yeshua was seen as the promised Messiah, as David's greater son. His followers were ready to reestablish the Davidic kingdom with Yeshua as Messiah. For this reason, they asked Him who would sit next to Him in His government cabinet (Matthew 19:28; 20:21). After the resurrection, they asked Yeshua if He would restore the kingdom to Israel at that time (Acts 1:6).

Much of Yeshua's teaching involved explanations to His disciples of the moral and spiritual (non-political) nature of His kingdom. It was *value-based, not power-based.* The community of Yeshua's followers was the advanced stage of historical process of the Jewish people who held the prophetic expectations of a Messianic kingdom. The first-century community of faith saw themselves as a continuation of the Israelite prophets.

This group of people became the carriers and protectors of the hope of the kingdom of God. When Shimon Kefa (Simon Peter) recognized that Yeshua was the Messiah, he was given the **"keys of the kingdom of heaven" (Matthew 16:19).** This was an endowment of enormous kingdom authority, almost like an appointment to a "cabinet" position.

Isaiah said that David had been given one key for the kingdom (Isaiah 22:22). Yeshua expanded what Isaiah said about David. In effect Yeshua

> *Much of Yeshua's teaching involved*
> *explanations to His disciples of the*
> *moral and spiritual (non-political) nature*
> *of His kingdom.*

was saying, "I am David's 'greater' son. I give you the same key that David had. Yet I give you many keys. David's key was for Israel alone. I give you keys to extend the kingdom to many other nations as well." This was an extension and expansion of the kingdom authority given to David.

It was an extension in the sense that it continues the covenants and prophecies given to Israel. It was an expansion in the sense that the many keys would include other nations and ethnic groups. It was also an "exaltation" of the kingdom in the sense that it affected the spiritual realms of angels in heaven as well as people on the earth.

The point is that Yeshua immediately executes an endowment of authority to His disciples. The delegation of authority from Yeshua to His disciples forms a chain of command to which we are to be aligned even today. Our alignment is not only a submission to God spiritually as individuals; it is also a submission to His delegated authority within the community of Yeshua's followers.

Yeshua formed a community (*ecclesia*) made up of those who followed Him (Matthew 16:18). He chose leaders among them (Luke 6:13). He gave those leaders authority. There was authority over demons (Luke 9:1; Mathew 10:1), authority within the community of faith (Matthew 16:19; 18:15–19) and, to a certain extent, to the whole world (John 20:23).

Yeshua is a king who came to set up a perfect kingdom (John 18:36–37). A king-dom is the "dom-inion" of the king. It is His realm of authority. Authority by its very nature is delegated through a chain of people (Luke 7:7–9). If we are to be aligned to Yeshua, we must be aligned to the delegated authority which He established. The kingdom of God can be defined as "the realm of Yeshua's authority." (Please see my book *All Authority* for further explanation of spiritual and delegated authority.)

> *Our alignment is not only a submission to God spiritually as individuals; it is also a submission to His delegated authority within the community of Yeshua's followers.*

The original twelve disciples were given the authority within Yeshua's kingdom. They and the others who followed them wrote the New Covenant Scriptures. All of us as believers in Yeshua receive the authority that was delegated to the original apostles of Yeshua. Those apostles and the Scriptures they wrote and the community they formed after Yeshua's resurrection comprise the original pattern to which we align ourselves today.

We see them as the continuation of the covenant family of Abraham, the priestly people of Moses, the kingdom nation of David, and the Messianic expectations of the Israelite prophets. In some ways, they were an alternative to the Greek, Roman, and Maccabean governments and an alternative to the Pharisee, Sadducee, and Essene religious groups.

As David replaced Saul as the true king, so did Yeshua replace those other political and religious groups. He invested His kingdom values and authority in those who followed after Him. In our view, they were the true Messianic community. The "kingdom" was in them.

We identify with them. We agree with their faith. We follow in their footsteps. We receive their authority. We model ourselves after their pattern. We align ourselves with their community. We aspire to complete what they started. It is interesting to see how many elements of the social and historical background surrounding that first-century community of faith have reappeared or been realigned in this century and in our generation.

Questions for Reflection

1. What was the historical background for the New Covenant during the fourth to first centuries BC?
2. What were the stages of the people of God before the time of the New Covenant community of faith?
3. What did it mean that Yeshua gave "keys" to Peter in Matthew 16?
4. What kind of people were the first followers of Yeshua?

4

Completing the Original Apostolic Commission

The community of the followers of Yeshua experienced a shocking transformation at the time of Yeshua's death and resurrection. For forty days after the Passover and before Pentecost (Shavuot), during the "counting of the Omer" (Leviticus 23), Yeshua gave instructions to His disciples about the kingdom of God (Acts 1:3).

This was more than just teaching the values of the kingdom as He did in the Sermon on the Mount. These were instructions from a king to his servants on how to spread and establish his government on the earth.

> *Now is the time for the international ecclesia to turn its attention back to Jerusalem as we seek to complete the Great Commission and get ready for the coming of Yeshua's kingdom.*

He tried to explain to them that the first step was for them to be filled with the power of the Holy Spirit (Acts 1:4–5). However, they were so excited about Him being the Messiah and establishing the Messianic kingdom that they could hardly hear what He had to say. They asked Him, **"Will You restore the kingdom to Israel at this time?" (Acts 1:6).** Restoring the kingdom to Israel is one of the primary themes of the whole Bible. They were stating what should have been obvious:

"You are the Messiah. You have died for our sins and risen from the dead. Now must be the time You will fulfill the covenant with David and the vision of the prophets. You will reform the religious system. You will

> ### *Restoring the kingdom to Israel is one of the primary themes of the whole Bible.*

drive out the tyrants from the Land. You will bring peace, prosperity, and righteousness. You will fulfill all the basic promises of the Bible." What could be clearer than that? What could be more central? What could be more comprehensive? This is the heart of the entire plan of God. Isn't it?

Well, Yeshua surprised them once again. Here is the commission of the apostles: **"It is not for you to know the times and the seasons set by the Father in His own authority. But you will receive power when the Holy Spirit comes upon you, and you will be witnesses of Me in Jerusalem, and all Judea and Samaria, even to the ends of the earth" (Acts 1:7–8).**

When Yeshua said they could not know the times set by the Father, He made a clear declaration that *there is indeed a time at which the kingdom will be restored to Israel* that will come at some point in history. In fact, that date has been set and pre-determined by God. The disciples did not make a mistake about the topic; they made a mistake about the timing. In retrospect, it is easy for us to see that the restoration of the kingdom to Israel comes at the end, not at the beginning.

Perhaps it would have been more logical for the kingdom to be established first in Israel and then go to the ends of the earth. However, Yeshua reversed the order. Timing sets an alignment. Yeshua is reversing the expected order. They were expecting Israel (totally), then the nations. Yeshua changed this to Israel (partially), then the nations, then Israel again at the end. (Or more exactly: Israel partially, Israel dispersed, gospel to the nations, Israel restored, Israel saved.) We need to conform ourselves to this timing and direction.

(Peter realizes later, in Acts 10:24, that all people are equal before God. Paul explains in Romans 11 that had the gospel not gone to the Gentiles before the restoration of Israel, then the peoples from the nations would have become second-class citizens in God's kingdom, and that is not God's way. The balancing act between Israel and the international church provides a way for everyone to have equal standing and destiny in God's kingdom.)

We have five new aspects of kingdom alignment here:

1. The gospel message will emanate from Jerusalem to the **ends of the earth.**

2. The kingdom will spread from Israel to the nations and then **back again.**

3. Israel will be **restored** at the **end** after having been destroyed for a long season.

4. **All the nations** of the earth will be included in Yeshua's kingdom government.

5. The full restoration of the kingdom will only occur when **Yeshua returns.**

It is interesting to note the difference between Yeshua's statements before and after the resurrection. In Matthew 10:6, Yeshua told His disciples to go only to the lost sheep of the house of Israel. In Acts 1:8, after the resurrection, He told them to go out to the Gentiles instead of staying in Israel. Another example: in Matthew 24:36, before the resurrection, Yeshua said that even He did not know the times set by the Father. In Acts 1:7, afterwards, He said that only His disciples are not to know.

We read these same words two thousand years later. We have come into the time of the end. God worked primarily in Israel for two thousand years from Abraham through the apostles. Then Israel was destroyed. Now, after another period of two thousand years, Israel has been restored as a nation. According to Yeshua's prophecy in **Luke 21:24 ("until the times of the Gentiles are fulfilled")**, the time of the Gentiles has come to its fullness. The time for the restoration of Israel has begun.

What a huge adjustment Yeshua's disciples had to make when He reversed the order of their expectations. They had to recalculate. They had to "restart their computers." They had to realign with His instructions.

Today the kingdom message is coming full circle. All of us as followers of Yeshua are called to *complete the apostolic commission*. What they started, the believers in the end times are to finish. We also have to make

> *What a huge adjustment Yeshua's disciples*
> *had to make when He reversed the order of*
> *their expectations.*

a huge adjustment, to recalculate. The first century was the time of the destruction of Israel. The twenty-first century is the time of the restoration of Israel. There is a reversal of strategy, a massive paradigm shift.

In some ways, there is no change at all. We just continue doing what they started. The world is round. As you keep going west, you eventually come back to the same point from the east (more on this in the chapters on "Global Alignment" and "Time and Geography"). Their generation went out from Jerusalem. Our generation comes back to Jerusalem. Their generation started the Great Commission. Our generation completes it.

When Yeshua told His disciples to be His witnesses to the ends of the earth, this meant that every individual from every nation would be invited to have forgiveness of sins and eternal life. Every human being is welcome in the kingdom of God. Every human being is to be warned of judgment and offered salvation before the day of judgment comes.

Actually, in Acts chapter 1, the words *salvation* or *gospel* are not mentioned. Of course, they are implied. However, the context of the chapter is the establishment of the kingdom (verses 3 and 6). When Yeshua spoke of the ends of the world, He was referring not only to the preaching of salvation but also to the extending of the borders of His kingdom.

His kingdom will not only be in Judea and Samaria like King David's, but it will extend all the way to the ends of the whole earth. It will be bigger than the Greek empire of Alexander the Great and bigger than the Roman empire of Julius Caesar. The background to the mission of Acts 1:8 to the "ends of the earth" is the vision of Isaiah and the other Israelite prophets.

In the last days the mountain of the Lord's house will be established at the head of the mountains and be lifted up above the hills; and all the nations will flow up to it. And many peoples will come and say, "Let us go up to the mountain of the Lord,

to the house of the God of Jacob; and He will teach us of His ways, and we will walk in His paths," for the Law will go out from Zion and the word of the Lord from Jerusalem. And He will judge between the nations and rebuke many peoples; and they will beat their swords into shovels and their spears into pruning shears. Nation will not lift up sword against nation; and they will not learn war anymore."

—Isaiah 2:2–4

I have made You as a covenant of the people, for a light of the nations.

—Isaiah 42:6

It is too light a thing for You to be My servant to raise up the tribes of Jacob and to restore the hidden ones of Israel; for I have given You as a light of the Gentiles, for My salvation to be to the ends of the earth.

—Isaiah 49:6

While Yeshua did not say "salvation" in Acts 1:8, He was obviously quoting **Isaiah 49:6**, which does say **"salvation to the ends of the earth."** I would interpret Yeshua's response to His disciples in Acts 1 as saying:

"You have asked Me to restore David's kingdom to Israel. The prophets envisioned a much wider kingdom which would cover the whole earth. Let's not settle for just David's kingdom; let's go for the whole vision of the prophets. Let's not set up the kingdom in Israel until we offer salvation to all the peoples of the earth. When they all have a chance to be part of the worldwide kingdom, let's return and restore the kingdom to Israel. The kingdom will start in Israel as Isaiah said, with its capital in Jerusalem, but it will cover the whole earth.

"I will establish the kingdom government on earth when I return. For now, proclaim both personal salvation and kingdom authority, from Jerusalem to the ends of the earth. In the meantime, there is no need for the nation of Israel to be here until it is time for My return and the kingdom restoration. Therefore, Israel will be scattered while the gospel goes to the Gentiles. Then in the period before I return, the nation will be restored, so that there will be a place for Me to return and set up the capital of My kingdom."

The **mission** of the apostles *is* the **vision** of the prophets.

In 2008, I had a unique opportunity to be interviewed in Hebrew on a full-length, well-known television program. At the end of the program, the interviewer asked me what our dream was as the Messianic community in Israel. After sharing my whole story of coming to believe in Yeshua, I ended the program by saying that our vision was the same as all the biblical prophets of Israel: to see the kingdom of Messiah established on earth.

One more aspect to this Great Commission was added by the angels to the apostles. **"Men of Galilee, why do you stand looking up into heaven? This Yeshua who was lifted up from you into heaven, He will return in the same way you have seen Him go up into heaven"** (Acts 1:11). It is clear that what the apostles asked about the kingdom being restored to Israel will take place when Yeshua returns from heaven to Jerusalem. The announcement by the angels about the return of Yeshua was the answer to their original question.

Yeshua returns to take up His kingdom on earth. He comes to conquer planet earth. As He came the first time as a sacrificial Lamb, He will return as a roaring Lion. We are to spread both the message of personal salvation by grace and the message of Yeshua's kingdom authority throughout the whole world right up to the time He returns.

Yeshua was quoting Isaiah that the Law would go out from Zion and that salvation should go to the ends of the earth. The Acts 1 mission is a grand enterprise to establish Isaiah's vision of a worldwide Messianic kingdom over the whole earth. Isaiah 2 is the context of Acts 1. The Acts 1 mission is to fulfill the Isaiah 2 vision.

When we started the Revive Israel team in 2004, we had in mind being a team like Yeshua and the Twelve. We had a group of about twelve young

Israelis. I wanted them to be trained as a new generation of disciples and apostles. We looked to Acts 1 as the perfect pattern. We started every day with praise-prayer-prophecy followed by some equipping-training-teaching. From there we set out to advance Yeshua's kingdom in whatever way we could.

We began to sense in prayer that the Lord was telling us: "I want you to adopt the Acts 1:8 commission *as if* it were yours." That didn't mean it was ours alone but that we were to adopt the vision in our hearts for full ownership and responsibility.

We didn't see how it could possibly be done. We said "yes" to the Lord, but it seemed totally impossible. We prayed for another full year to try to understand what to do and how to do it. Finally, we discerned the Lord saying, "The way to fulfill the Acts 1 mission is by the Isaiah 2 vision."

This meant to us three clear steps of operation:

1. Send out teachings to the whole world on **media** ("Out of Zion will go forth the law")
2. Send out members of our team on short-term ministry **trips** to various locations around the world ("and the word of the Lord from Jerusalem")
3. Receive **guests** as visitors; pray for them; teach them; build relationships; send them back home with blessing ("Many people will come and say, 'Let us go up…'").

We had to increase our faith to embrace such a large vision. We had to enlarge our hearts to see the Gentile nations as part of our calling. We had to adjust our direction to see the word of the Lord going out from Zion. We had to adjust our direction to see the nations coming up to us. This was a huge realignment in our hearts, and way beyond our ability. But, of course, with God all things are possible by His grace.

The command of Yeshua to go from Jerusalem to the ends of the earth sets a linear "mapping" of His kingdom plan. It sets Jerusalem as its capital, as juxtaposed to Rome as the capital of Caesar's government. The Book of Acts starts in Jerusalem and ends up in Rome. However, we believe that the kingdom returns to Jerusalem at Yeshua's return. (Paul Liberman wrote in his book, *The Fig Tree Blossoms*, that it is as if the general pattern is going backwards now from Acts 28 to Acts 1.)

This is our part in the original apostolic commission. What they started, we finish. They went out from Jerusalem; we come back to Jerusalem. As there was a major paradigm shift in the generation right after Yeshua's first coming, so is there a major shift in the generation right before His second coming.

Now is the time to shift. The alignment is coming back to Jerusalem. Now is the time for the international ecclesia to turn its attention back to Jerusalem as we seek to complete the Great Commission and get ready for the coming of Yeshua's kingdom.

This is our alignment. Will we complete what the first apostles started? Can we work together and dedicate ourselves to finish this great plan? We can't do it without you, and you can't do it without us. Let's come into alignment and do it together.

Questions for Reflection

1. What did the disciples understand and what did they not understand when they asked, **"Will You at this time restore the kingdom to Israel" (Acts 1:6)?**

2. What did Yeshua mean when He said to be witnesses **"to the ends of the earth" (Acts 1:8)?**

3. What is the connection between the gospel commission of the apostles and the kingdom vision of the prophets?

4. How are we to complete the apostolic commission in our generation?

5

Transferring the Kingdom From Heaven to Earth

Ultimately the Great Commission ends with the return of Yeshua and the kingdom of God being established on earth. Strangely enough, the very concept of the kingdom of God on planet earth is foreign to many, or at least not well-understood.

Here is the central prayer for the coming of the kingdom, as Yeshua taught us:

> *Ultimately the Great Commission ends with the return of Yeshua and the kingdom of God being established on earth.*

Your kingdom come; Your will be done on earth as it is in heaven.

—Matthew 6:10

Notice that this kingdom has an origin, a direction, and a destination:

1. Origin: Heaven
2. Direction: Heaven to Earth
3. Destination: Earth.

This gives us very clear instructions. What is the problem? What is the challenge on a practical level? It is the human will. The will of God is already done in heaven. It is not being done on earth. The will of God is not being done by human beings. The key change that has to take place is a change in the will of human beings.

Yeshua asked His disciples to pray with Him, **"Not my will but Yours**

We study and pray so that we can understand God's will.

be done" **(Matthew 26:39)**. One thing that should happen in prayer is that we change our will. We study and pray so that we can understand God's will. Because the human race is generally going in the wrong direction, God's will usually seems to be directly opposed to what we want.

Yeshua said of Jerusalem, **"How many times I wanted to gather you together...but you were not willing" (Matthew 23:37)**. He wanted; we didn't. God has a good will and purpose for us, but most of the time we are not willing. We don't want it; we even rebel against it. God wants to give us peace, prosperity, and even power but says **"you were not willing"** and **"you chose what I did not desire" (Isaiah 30:15, 65:12)**.

When we pray, we change our wills to fit God's will. We wrestle our wills into submission. That is how we bring the kingdom of God to earth. We change our will to align with His. When enough human beings have changed their will to God's will, then the kingdom of God will manifest across the whole earth.

As Isaiah 2 is the context for "Go into all the world," so is Daniel 7 the context for "Your kingdom come!"

Daniel 7 describes four evil kingdoms (beasts) that have dominion over the earth (verses 1–8). God judges them and promises that a new kingdom of righteousness will replace them. The replacement of the evil kingdoms with the good kingdom is a process that goes through several stages and takes much time to be completed (verses 9–12).

The determining factor of this kingdom replacement is that a righteous hero, called "the son of man," will receive authority from God to take over the world. **"Behold, one like the son of man came on the clouds of heaven, and he came up to the Ancient of days, and brought near to Him. Dominion, glory, and a kingdom were given to him; and all the people, nations and dominions worshiped him. His dominion will be an everlasting dominion and his kingdom will not be taken away** or end" **(Daniel 7:13–14)**. This is Messiah Yeshua Himself receiving the kingdom of God.

The first thing He does is delegate and transfer authority to a group of people called "the saints." **"The saints of the Most High will receive the kingdom, and they will possess the kingdom forever" (Daniel 7:18).** Notice that there are two verbs here: The first verb is to receive, the second is to possess. The word for "receive" in Aramaic is simply *y'kablun* יקבלון. The second verb means to take hold of by strength, *y'khasnun* יחסנון. It is the root for the modern Hebrew word meaning "muscular, strong, protected" and even "a medical immunization."

These two words represent two stages in the transfer of kingdom authority. First it must be received spiritually in the heart. Then later, after much battle, it is put into place outwardly. This is how the kingdom works. First there is spiritual authority in the heart. Later it becomes governmental authority in the world.

Once the saints "receive" spiritual authority, the evil kingdoms of the world attack them and even **"make war against the saints" (verse 21).** This is spiritual warfare. The persecution against the saints is so bad that it actually **"overcomes them" (verse 21).** This is the "in-between" time in which we live now. Evil forces dominate the world. A small minority of good-hearted people have received spiritual authority to rule the world in the future. In the meantime, the evil forces attack them, make war against them, and even overcome them.

This is the paradox of the present age. There is good, but the evil in the world wages war against it and often seems to be winning. The righteous suffer.

But this in-between time does not last forever. It comes to an end. Then there is another time when God intervenes, punishes the evil, and the government of the world is turned over to the righteous to actualize and take possession of the kingdom. **"Until the Ancient of Days comes and gives justice for the saints of the Most High; and the time has come for the saints to take possession of the kingdom" (verse 22).**

Notice the word *time* in this verse: the time to take possession comes after the time of persecution which comes after the time of receiving kingdom authority. [The **"time for the saints to take possession of the kingdom"** in **Daniel 7:22** is essentially the same time for Yeshua to **"restore the kingdom to Israel"** as requested by the disciples in **Acts 1:6**. That is the **"set time"** to **"favor Zion" (Psalm 102:13)**.]

Let's put this progression in forward motion:

1. Evil kingdoms rule the earth.

2. Son of Man receives authority.

3. Spiritual authority is given to the saints.

4. War (and persecution) is made against the saints.

5. Saints take possession of the kingdom.

There is a time to receive spiritual authority, there is a time to stand in persecution, and there is a time to take possession of the government on earth.

Daniel's prophecy goes on to give details about the timing. The war and persecution against the saints becomes more intense until the time right before the end. Then there will be an evil leader who will lead the great persecution and intense tribulation against the saints for a period of three and a half years (verse 25). Then the evil kingdoms are judged and destroyed (verse 26). Then the saints take dominion over the earth forever (verse 27).

You may have to read Daniel 7 several times to grasp its clarity and its power. Daniel's prophecies must be kept in mind when reading the end times' prophecies of the New Covenant, because the New Covenant writers had his prophecies in mind when they wrote. They saw themselves as continuing, clarifying, and elaborating on what Daniel wrote.

[Actually, Daniel said that he didn't understand all the prophecies that he wrote. God told him they would be understood far in the future by the people who would live in the end times. For Daniel, it was sealed (Daniel 8:26; 12:4, 9); for us the seals are beginning to open.]

Let's simplify our role even more to just three stages:

1. *Receiving* spiritual power to reign.

> ### *Spiritual authority within the community of saints before the second coming transitions to government authority over the nations after the second coming.*

2. *Standing* in spiritual warfare, suffering, and persecution.

3. *Possessing* government authority on the earth.

One could make a mistake on any one of these three points. Those mistakes would logically be:

1. We never will take possession of earth—just live in heaven (mystic dualism).

2. We do not have to go through persecution and tribulation (pre-tribulation).

3. We will take full possession of the earth during this present time before the intervention of God in the end time (dominion now).

These are not merely issues of theological theories but of kingdom strategy. We are already entering the end times. We don't want to make mistakes in how we prepare ourselves.

The Christian worldview has tended to be a heaven-only kingdom. The Jewish worldview has tended to be an earth-only kingdom. The Bible speaks of the kingdom as uniting all things in heaven *and* earth. **"The heavens are My throne and the earth is My footstool" (Isaiah 66:1)** is a poetic way to say it. (See also: Genesis 1:1; Psalm 115:16; Matthew 6:10, 19:28; Romans 8:19–21; Ephesians 1:10; Colossians 1:16). We want both dimensions.

At the crucifixion, Yeshua obtained forgiveness of sins for us. At the resurrection, He gave us eternal life. At the ascension, He obtained authority for us. At Pentecost, He gave us the power of the Holy Spirit to walk in righteousness (Romans 8:4). At the second coming, the kingdoms of this world will be turned over to Yeshua and to the people who have learned to walk in that righteousness (Romans 5:17; Matthew 19:28).

Spiritual authority within the community of saints before the second coming transitions to government authority over the nations after the second coming.

The principle is spiritual authority now; government authority later (and moral opposition in the meantime). There is a steady progression from spiritual authority to government authority. Our emphasis is on the moral values to be able to rule correctly, not on the executive power to make other people obey.

God has unlimited power and authority. What is lacking is people with Christlike character. By faith we should be gaining more of the kind of authority that blesses and helps others—wisdom, experience, patience, humility, and righteousness—with each passing day. Moral and spiritual opposition in this life enables us to grow in those character qualities.

Kingdom authority and righteousness is always growing (see the "seed" parables of Matthew 13 and Mark 4). The more that righteous people can receive authority now in business, government, and religion, the more the kingdom of God will advance in our lifetime.

Kingdom alignment includes the continual transfer of spiritual authority from heaven to earth now until, **with the return of Yeshua,** it becomes the full government authority in the future. The kingdom is already in our hearts, yet it grows gradually through the spread of the gospel until it takes over the earth **when Yeshua returns** (Matthew 13:32, 33; Mark 4:26–32).

The kingdom grows gradually in the present until there is a moment of dramatic change at the end. That is the moment of the "sickle" (harvest) at the coming of Yeshua (Mark 4:29; Revelation 14:15). There is both a gradual process now and a sudden moment at the end. Kingdom government is partial in this lifetime and full in the world to come.

Apostolic authority in the ecclesia becomes the government authority in the kingdom. **"I say to you who have followed after Me; at the renewal of creation when the son of man sits upon His throne of glory, you also will sit on twelve thrones to judge the twelve tribes of Israel" (Matthew 19:28).** The twelve apostles become twelve kings ruling under the King of kings.

> *Everything in this life, no matter how small,*
> *is a test of faithfulness to determine how much*
> *authority you will have in the life to come.*

However, these are not the only positions of government. There are other countries and other levels of authority. **"Well done, good servant! Because you were faithful in very little, have authority of ten cities"** (Luke 19:17). **"And He said also to this one, 'You will be over five cities'"** (verse 19). The potential to rule is given by grace. However, the worthiness to rule is proven over a lifetime of faithfulness and serving.

Everything in this life, no matter how small, is a test of faithfulness to determine how much authority you will have in the life to come. Authority and responsibility go together. **"Those who have received the abundance of grace and the gift of righteousness will reign in life because of one, Messiah Yeshua"** (**Romans 5:17**). *Righteousness* is a gift of grace which is given as a seed; it is also a fruit of the Spirit which is grown over time.

At the very moment of *creation*, God made human beings to share dominion with Him over His creation (Genesis 1:26). This will come to pass in Yeshua's kingdom.

1. On earth: **"He has made us… kings and priests and we will reign on the earth"** (**Revelation 5:10**).

2. For a thousand years: **"They will reign with Him a thousand years"** (**Revelation 20:6**).

3. For eternity: **"They will reign forever and ever"** (**Revelation 22:5**).

The prophetic plan for the coming of the kingdom is revealed in stages. The last secret is revealed at the seventh trumpet (Revelation 10:7). That final mystery is that the governments of this world will be taken over by Yeshua at His coming. **"The kingdoms of this world have become the kingdom of our Lord and of His Messiah; and He will reign forever and ever"** (**Revelation 11:15**).

His kingdom really will come. It will *come* from heaven. **"May Your kingdom come; May Your will be done on earth as it is in heaven" (Matthew 6:10)**. Spiritual authority and moral values are being transferred from heaven to earth. It has already come in our hearts. Eventually God's will and righteousness will be done on earth. We are to align ourselves with that kingdom and that *righteousness*. **"Seek first the kingdom of God and His righteousness" (Matthew 6:33)**. That is our heart's desire.

The plan for restoring dominion comes in **stages**. In this lifetime we are to restore the *hearts* of human beings to God and to have *godly influence* on human society around us.

Then Yeshua will return. He will rule for a thousand years in order to restore God's will to this planet. We are destined to rule together with Him in the *government* of the Messianic millennial kingdom.

After a thousand years, the entire *creation* will be renewed, and God's total and perfect dominion will be restored for eternity (Revelation 21–22).

Let us summarize these three states of dominion.

1. **Present:** Spiritual dominion through prayer and touching people's hearts by the love and truth of the gospel; positive *influence* on society around us as much as possible.

2. **Millennium:** At Yeshua's return, human society will be restored with righteous *government* led by Yeshua for a thousand years.

3. **Eternity**: Perfect *paradise* restored; heaven and earth reunited; creation renewed into God's original plan.

Our dominion in Yeshua is now spiritual and moral; when Yeshua returns it will be governmental. Ultimately the restoration will be cosmic, glorious, and perfect.

Questions for Reflection

1. What is the origin, direction, and destination of God's kingdom?
2. How could you summarize the transfer of authority to the saints in Daniel 7?
3. Is there a difference between "receiving" the kingdom and "possessing" it?
4. How does spiritual authority now turn into government authority in the world to come?
5. How is the characteristic of righteousness a prerequisite for ruling and reigning?

6

Preparing for the Second Coming

With every passing day, we move further away from the crucifixion and closer to His coming. The second coming provides a clear marker to which all of us should be aligned. He will come back to a certain place at a certain time. There are events that must take place leading up to that time. The cross is our point of orientation from the past. The second coming is our point of orientation for the future.

Part of our international mission statement at Tikkun Global is: **to prepare the church to stand with Israel during the difficult events leading up to the second coming.**

> *The second coming is fully physical.*
> *There will be a real war, a real earthquake,*
> *and a real reentry into Jerusalem.*

Both the crucifixion of Yeshua and the second coming occur in Jerusalem. Thus, the physical location of Jerusalem will have significance once again. Both events have to take place in Jerusalem. For most of the past two thousand years, from AD 70 to AD 1967, Jerusalem has not had so much importance as a geographical center of kingdom strategy. The city had been destroyed and left desolate.

The destruction of Jerusalem and its future restoration were predicted clearly by Yeshua in what was perhaps the single greatest predictive prophecy in history.

> *With every passing day,*
> *we move further away from the crucifixion*
> *and closer to His coming.*

They will fall by the sword and be exiled into all the nations; and Jerusalem will be trampled underfoot by the Gentiles until the times of the Gentiles are fulfilled.

—Luke 21:24

The destruction and rebuilding of Jerusalem were foretold. The rebuilding of Jerusalem is seen as a transition of spiritual importance marking the fullness of the times of the Gentiles. Jerusalem is the indicator of the change in the timing of God's plan.

What is the significance of the times of the Gentiles? What is the period after the end of the times of the Gentiles? The biblical nickname for Jerusalem is Zion, *Tsiyon*, ציון. The word *Zion* means signpost. A signpost points to something. It is a sign; it has *sign-ificance*. What is the reestablishment of the city of Jerusalem pointing to?

For the past two thousand years, the priorities in God's plan have been to bring the gospel to every nation, to build the international ecclesia, and to spread the presence of the Holy Spirit. For these three goals (gospel, church, Holy Spirit), there is no need of a specific location. The Holy Spirit can be poured out at any time and any place. The ecclesia is found in every nation. Every person is invited to receive salvation at any time.

The Spirit is not limited to time and space. However, Yeshua is a man who lives in a body. He is confined to time and space when He is in this world. He had to be crucified in a specific place at a specific time. When He returns, He will return to a specific place at a specific time. That place is Jerusalem. Jerusalem did not have geographic importance for the past two thousand years. During that period of time, it was also not so important for Yeshua to be physically located on earth.

Jerusalem had to be in position for the events of the first coming. The fact that Jerusalem has been restored means that we are being prepared

> ### *The cross is our point of orientation from the past. The second coming is our point of orientation for the future.*

for the second coming. Jerusalem is the city of Yeshua. It was founded by Yeshua's great-great grandfather, David. Yeshua is the greater Son of David, the ruler and heir apparent of the city.

Nir Barkat, previous mayor of Jerusalem, claims to have direct descent from King David (although no one can prove that today). In any case, he felt an identification with David. He believed he had a destiny to restore the city that his forefather built. How much more so could we say that of Yeshua Himself!

One of the members of the Messianic community in Israel is a dear friend, Hanoch Maoz, who was one of the frontline soldiers who broke through to the Temple Mount in the Six-Day War of 1967. The fact that he survived, while many of his friends were killed around him, was one of the reasons that made him search for God and eventually come to faith in Yeshua.

He tells the story that after the war he read and identified with **Psalm 122:2**, which says, **"Our feet were standing in your gates, O Jerusalem."** I jokingly replied to him, "Yes, but it didn't say you were going to have to blow up the gate with dynamite on the way in." (He also tells how they had brought enough explosives to blow up the Al Aqsa mosque, but they were given instructions not to do so by Moshe Dayan.)

In Acts 1:9–12 we studied earlier that Yeshua ascended from the Mount of Olives and that the angels said He would return the same way. There is a line going up and a line coming back down. That line goes from earthly Jerusalem to heavenly Jerusalem and back down again.

It is not the purpose of this book to teach about prophecies of the end times. (We have other teaching materials on that subject.) Here the point is to show that the second coming at Jerusalem forms a solid marker stone for our current alignment as the people of God. The starting line and the finish line is Jerusalem.

[It is interesting that the word *Judaism* does not appear even *one* time in the entire Tanakh (Old Testament); the word *Christianity* does not appear even *one* time in the New Covenant; and the word *Jerusalem* does not appear even *one* time in the Koran.]

In Revelation 19:11–19 we find the clearest description of Yeshua descending from heaven at the second coming. There it is stated that He comes as a warrior general, with fire and anger, to destroy the forces of the anti-Christ. His eyes are flames of fire; He is riding a white horse, leading an army of warrior angels.

All the descriptions of the end times in the Hebrew prophets culminate in a great war in which the nations of the world attack Jerusalem. The clearest of them is **Zechariah 14:1–5**:

הִנֵּה יוֹם־בָּא לַיהוה וְחֻלַּק שְׁלָלֵךְ בְּקִרְבֵּךְ;

וְאָסַפְתִּי אֶת־כָּל־הַגּוֹיִם אֶל־יְרוּשָׁלַ͏ִם לַמִּלְחָמָה וְנִלְכְּדָה הָעִיר... אַצְיָן יַצָּא חֲצִי הָעִיר בַּגּוֹלָה
וְיֶתֶר הָעָם לֹא יִכָּרֵת מִן־הָעִיר:

וְיָצָא יהוה וְנִלְחַם בַּגּוֹיִם הָהֵם כְּיוֹם הִלָּחֲמוֹ בְּיוֹם קְרָב:

וְעָמְדוּ רַגְלָיו בַּיּוֹם־הַהוּא עַל־הַר הַזֵּתִים אֲשֶׁר עַל־פְּנֵי יְרוּשָׁלַ͏ִם מִקֶּדֶם וְנִבְקַע הַר
הַזֵּיתִים

... וּבָא יהוה אֱלֹהַי כָּל־קְדֹשִׁים עִמָּךְ;

1. **Behold a day is coming to YHVH and your spoil will be divided in your midst.**

2. **I will gather all the nations to Jerusalem to war; and the city will be captured...and half the city will go out into exile and the rest of the people will not be cut off from the city.**

3. **And YHVH will go forth and fight against those nations as in the day when He makes war in the day of battle...**

4. **And His feet will stand on that day upon the Mount of Olives which faces Jerusalem on the east, and the Mount of Olives will be split in two...**

5. **And YHVH my God will come; and all the saints will be with you.**

This prophecy has several elements:

– **"the day of YHVH" (verse 1)**.

– **"All the nations will be gathered to Jerusalem to battle" (verse 2)**.

– **"Half of the city will be cut off" (verse 2)**.

– **"YHVH will go out and fight against those nations" (verse 3)**.

– **"His feet will stand on that day on the Mount of Olives which faces Jerusalem on the east" (verse 4)**.

– **"The Mount of Olives will be split in two" (verse 4)**.

– **"YHVH will come and all of the holy ones with Him (verse 5)**.

This is a stunningly specific and graphic description of the second coming. Since verse 4 says that the "feet of YHVH" will touch the Mount of Olives, we know that this must be Yeshua (having feet and being called YHVH); that the second coming is fully physical; and that there will be a real war, a real earthquake, and a real reentry into Jerusalem.

All the nations will come against Jerusalem. Yeshua will fight against them. This creates a clear dividing line spiritually, politically, historically, and even theologically. At the day of the second coming, everyone will be found fighting against Yeshua or for Him. There will be no middle ground.

The dividing line described here is not primarily a declaration of faith in Yeshua. The nations fighting against Jerusalem may not even realize they are fighting against Yeshua. It may be a coalition of Islam, ecumenical Judeo-Christianity, the United Nations, Communists, secular humanists, etc.—fighting against the "fundamentalism" of evangelical Christians and Zionist Jews. Or it might be a more politically/economically/motivated attack.

There will be a worldwide realignment. It will be made up of those Bible-believing Christians who recognize God's covenant with Israel and of a major part of the people of Israel. It will likely include as well good-hearted humanists who are outraged by the huge injustice being done to evangelical Christians and to the nation of Israel. This coalition will stand up against the injustice, but they will be a minority.

The majority of nations, including faithless Jews and Christians, will be swept away in this deception. They will be flooded with media lies about world peace and a one-world religion. They will hate true Christians and true Jews. It will be like World War II and the Holocaust, but much greater. In this huge war evil forces will try to conquer Israel and all the nations. It will include a campaign to persecute and murder Jews and Christians.

In this massive apocalyptic war, apparently one-third of the entire human race will be slaughtered (Revelation 9:15, 18), two-thirds of the nation of Israel (Zechariah 13:8), and one-half of Jerusalem (14:2). At that moment, there is no room for any more delay. The punishment and judgment of God will be released against the wicked like a flash of lightning.

Although the majority of the nations will be aligned in this coalition against Israel and the church, there will be another alignment with Israel and the church standing together. This alignment has already started. Everyone in the world will be on one side or the other.

The linchpin between the international ecclesia and the nation of Israel is the Messianic Jewish remnant. The Messianic remnant is part of Israel by nationhood, language, history, and ethnicity. It is part of the ecclesia by faith in Messiah Yeshua, new birth, indwelling of the Holy Spirit, and loving fellowship.

The international ecclesia will be aligned with Israel in the end times. This alignment comes by partnership with the Messianic community within Israel. The partnership takes place by covenantal relationship, common faith, and an understanding of biblical prophecy.

It is the "One New Man" of Ephesians 2 and the "Olive Tree" of Romans 11 that form the true alignment. Let us build that partnership. It is the essential bond of faith between Israel and the church that leads to the coming of Yeshua's kingdom on the earth. He is both the head of the church (Ephesians 1:22) and the King of Israel (John 12:13).

We have been searching for the right word for "alignment" in Hebrew. Normally we say, יישור קו *yishur kav*, which means "straightening out towards a line." One morning at prayer time, my friend Youval Yanay sug-

> ## *The fact that Jerusalem has been restored means that we are being prepared for the second coming.*

gested another word which was on my heart as well: *he'arkhut*, הֵיעָרְכוּת. This is a somewhat literary word, and it has several meanings.

The first meaning of *he'arkhut* is just what we have said here. It means "to be aligned and arranged in a certain order." However, it also means to be "arrayed for battle." This would fit the double meaning perfectly. There will be a righteous unity and alignment with Israel and the church. And there will be an evil, anti-Christ alignment that will incite all the nations to attack Israel and kill Jews and Christians.

(In World War II, many innocent people were killed from all different kinds of backgrounds. In the recent waves of Islamic terrorism and Jihad, more innocent Muslims have been killed than people of any other background. It would be logical that in the horrible, apocalyptic wars of the end times, many innocent people will be killed from all types of backgrounds, not just evangelical Christians and Zionist Jews.)

This Hebrew word for alignment is taken from the word *arukh*, עָרוּךְ, meaning "prepared." It is like a **"table prepared for me in the presence of my enemies" (Psalm 23:5)** and the **"race set before me" (Hebrews 12:1)**. It means "to set in order."

So there is a **double alignment**: one for war in which all the nations will come against Jerusalem to battle; the other as an alignment between Israel and the church, with the covenant link being the Messianic remnant. Now is the time to form this alliance. Now is the time to build this alignment. It is urgent. Millions of lives are at stake.

The clash of the centuries is about to take place. **"The kings of the earth have taken their stand; and the princes have taken counsel together, against the Lord and against His Messiah" (Psalm 2:2)**. This is the coalition of evil, murder, and rebellion. But God laughs in derision and says, **"I have set My king on My holy mountain Zion" (Psalm 2:6)**.

The coalition of the righteous forms an alignment around these two points: God's king (Yeshua) and God's city (Jerusalem).

Yeshua is a King. Jerusalem will be the capital of His kingdom. The capital represents His governmental authority. The forces of evil will seek to destroy the King, the King's capital, and all those who join with them. The double alignment is starting now. Let's make sure we are on the right side.

Questions for Reflection

1. What did Yeshua predict about the destruction and rebuilding of Jerusalem in Luke 21?
2. What is the root meaning of the name Zion?
3. What is the difference in point of view between Zechariah 14 and Revelation 19?
4. What would have to take place in order for "all the nations" to attack Jerusalem?
5. What is the "double alignment," both positive and negative, about the nations coming to Jerusalem?

7

Prerequisites for the Second Coming

The day of the second coming of Yeshua represents the ultimate focal point for this stage of the kingdom of God. It is the finish line of the race we are running. Many events lead up to that moment. However, there are three significant prophecies, or "prerequisites," that are a type of prelude to that grand finale:

1. Gospel: In **Matthew 24:14**, Yeshua said He would not return until **"This gospel of the kingdom is preached in all the world."**

2. Jerusalem: In **Matthew 23:39**, Yeshua said He would not return until the people of Jerusalem welcomed Him back with cries of **"Barukh Haba"—"Blessed is He who comes"—"הבא בשם ה ברוך"**.

3. Bride: In **Revelation 19:7**, right before the coming of the Lord, we notice that **"The Bride has made herself ready."**

> *How exciting and brilliant it is that God's plan is brought about by the partnership and interdependence between Israel and the church!*

[Note: When we say prerequisites, we mean that these are conditions set in Scripture by the sovereignty of God, certainly not prerequisites that God is required to do that we think are right. We are submitted to His conditions, not the other way around.]

> *The day of the second coming of Yeshua rep-resents the ultimate focal point for this stage of the kingdom of God.*

These three "tracks" must come to their fullness. The gospel of the kingdom must be preached to all people. The Jewish people must come to a point of revival to cry out to the Lord. The ecclesia church "Bride" must come to full maturity and purity.

Let's try to hone it down to:

1. Gospel of the kingdom

2. Revival in Israel

3. Fullness of the church.

In the viewpoint of Scripture, there is a three-fold cord consisting of Israel, the church, and the kingdom. They are linked together. They affect one another. They come to their fullness together. Ultimately, they become one together.

Gospel of the Kingdom

The gospel of the kingdom includes all the elements of God's plan, starting with personal repentance and continuing until the establishment of the kingdom of God on earth. Yeshua came the first time to give personal salvation. He comes the second time to establish His kingdom on earth.

Since Yeshua returns to establish His kingdom, it is not enough to teach only personal salvation; we must teach all the dimensions of the kingdom. God's people must know about kingdom principles in order to be part of cooperating with Yeshua when He comes. If the goal was only personal salvation, there would be no reason for Yeshua to return. People could simply die and go to heaven.

His return is not for salvation but for the kingdom. In order for Him to return, all nations should have had a chance to hear about salvation and the kingdom. And as well, believers must be trained in kingdom righteousness. That righteousness must be in us before it can be transferred to the world. That is why we teach and preach about the kingdom.

Revival in Israel

Revival in Israel is such a central theme to us that we named our discipleship ministry team "Revive Israel." We are on the way to a major revival in Israel, and that revival leads to a cry of welcoming Yeshua to return as King. All of us in our Tikkun Global family have been serving this vision for decades. We believe in the fulfillment of the promise **"All Israel will be saved" (Romans 11:26)**. In fact, that is the heart of Messianic Jews anywhere.

This moment of revival and receiving the Messiah is the culmination of the history of the Jewish people. It is a process involving many parts. The people have to be brought back from the two-thousand-year exile. The language has to be restored, the nation restored, and the capital restored.

The nation must be prayed for, the gospel preached, congregations established, and new believers discipled. The Messianic community must come to a maturity. There must be spiritual leadership, including all the five-fold ministry gifts (Ephesians 4:11–16). There must be cooperation between the remnant of Israel and the international ecclesia.

The people of Israel as a whole are going through a process of spiritual searching. The political, financial, philosophical, and religious options are being tried and found lacking. In the end, many secular and religious Jews will turn to Yeshua. This will occur during a time of extreme turmoil and tribulation. It will be a cry for help.

Fullness of the Church

The international ecclesia is going through its own process. She is described as a "Bride." She is getting "ready." There is purity, desire, and maturity. There must be a remnant community of faith in every nation with prayer, praise, solid Bible teaching, unity, and anointed leadership.

The Book of Revelation gives a spiritual picture of this glorified bride in Revelation 12:1. The bride goes through the difficult events of the end times and then is described as finally having made herself ready (Revelation 19:7). Chapters 12 through 19 may be seen as the final stages of the people of God being made ready for the second coming.

As this international ecclesia Bride comes to her fullness, there will also be a revelation of the place and calling of Israel. Understanding the church will be the last mystery for Israel. Understanding Israel will be the last mystery for the church. Paul makes this statement that the fullness of the international Gentile church comes at the same time that the church receives revelation about Israel:

"I do not want you to be ignorant of this mystery lest you be wise in your own eyes: hardness of heart has happened in part to Israel until the fullness of the Gentiles comes in. And so all Israel will be saved" (Romans 11:25–26).

I hope you can see the basic elements of these verses:

1. Gentile church fullness

2. Church revelation about Israel

3. Israel saved as result.

As the church comes to her fullness, she has a revelation about Israel. As she prays for Israel, the revival in Israel begins. Then all Israel will be saved. Israel will call out for Yeshua to come. Then the kingdom of God will be established on earth. It all starts with the church praying for Israel's salvation (Romans 9:1–5; 10:1–2).

The fullness of the church leads to Israel's revival. The fullness of Israel leads to the coming of the kingdom. How exciting and brilliant it is that God's plan is brought about by the partnership and interdependence between Israel and the church (Romans 11:33)!

The Triple Play

When we perceive these three parts of God's plan—Israel, the church, and the kingdom—lining up together in our own hearts, we know we are rightly aligned to His purposes. We understand that these three are connected, and we serve the purposes of all three.

When we talk about "global alignment," we are talking about the church being aligned with Israel for the sake of the kingdom. It cannot start with Israel's revival. Romans 11:25 speaks of the church understanding God's purposes for Israel. Romans 11:26 says, "And so" all Israel will be saved. Verse 25 comes before verse 26. The revelation of the church about Israel is what opens the door for Israel to be saved.

Israel cannot be saved without the prayer intercession of the church. No nation, including Israel, can save itself. Israel's salvation can only come from those who already have salvation. Israel cannot pray enough for herself. It is the Gentile church that must pray for Israel. Israel is dependent on the church to receive this spiritual revival.

In a similar way, the church's desire for the coming of Yeshua is dependent on Israel. God made a covenant with David that the kingdom of God on earth belongs to his seed. Israel has the covenant rights to invite Yeshua to return and reign as king. As David received the kingdom government by affirmation of the elders of Judah, so will Yeshua's taking up the throne be affirmed by some kind of spiritual parallel to the ancient Judean elders.

Yeshua will return to rule and reign over David's kingdom. The call for Yeshua to return is not only a welcoming invitation but an inauguration for Yeshua to lead the government. The cry of "Blessed is He who comes" is to affirm and inaugurate Yeshua as king over the earthly kingdom, which was given to David and his seed by divine covenant.

Israel is dependent on the church for salvation; the church is dependent on Israel to bring Yeshua's kingdom.

Worldwide Prayer for Israel

In 1980 I had an unusual spiritual experience at the Temple Mount Wall in Jerusalem. I was praying wearing the traditional Jewish garments, including *tefillin* leather straps (phylacteries). I began to pray in Hebrew and in tongues as I touched the Wall. I felt in my spirit that something like a waterfall of light was coming down off the Temple Mount over my head. The waterfall of light came slowly, as if it was made out of honey.

When it touched my head, I had a moment where I was "in the spirit" so to speak. There was a "discernment of spirits" in which I could see what looked like fortresses surrounding the city of Jerusalem. I heard in my heart the Lord say, "Even if you and all the Messianic Jews do everything you can, you will not be able to bring revival to the city." I perceived that the fortresses were evil strongholds, made up primarily of "religious spirits." I realized how strong the demonic opposition was toward revival taking place in Israel.

I cried out to the Lord for an answer. I again heard Him speak in my heart, this time saying, "The only way you will succeed in bringing salvation to your people will be *if Christians in every nation of the world will pray* for this to happen." The impact of this vision on my soul was enormous, and its implications seemed to me beyond what words could describe.

Mike Bickle of International House of Prayer shared with us at a conference for Tikkun ministries, together with Dan Juster, Paul Wilbur, and Eitan Shishkoff. Mike told the story of how an uneducated farmer named Bob Jones showed up at his office in 1983 to tell him that he would one day lead a movement of young people around the world committed to 24/7 prayer and praise.

Bob also told him that he saw in the future people joining in this prayer even in rice paddies in the Far East, watching Mike on what looked like small, wireless television screens which they were able to hold in the palms of their hands. Bob also told Mike that this prayer network would ultimately be used to *intercede for Israel in the end times.*

Kansas City was seen as being a spiritually significant location because it was the city of Harry Truman, president of the United States when Israel became a state in 1948. Truman was the first world leader to recognize the State of Israel. Truman could be seen as representing the covenantal relationship between Israel and the US. Bob said that one day this worldwide prayer ministry would have its base at the Truman farm property on the outskirts of Kansas City.

This seemed totally preposterous to Mike, and yet over the years it has all miraculously come to pass. An unusual divine intervention in this whole saga is the acquiring of the Truman farm property. This is a large property worth millions of dollars. Mike didn't see any way for this part of the prophecy to come to pass.

The Trumans sold their farm to a local Jewish family named Goldberg on January 27, 1958. Their daughter, Lynn, inherited the property. Lynn then married William Intrater (a distant unknown relative). In an extraor-

> *Israel is dependent on the church for salvation; the church is dependent on Israel to bring Yeshua's kingdom.*

dinary act of generosity, they sold/donated the property to IHOP-KC. The closing was January 27, 2008—exactly fifty years later, to the day! (The new IHOP-KC center on the Truman property was dedicated in May 2022.)

There has been supernatural intervention throughout the history of IHOP-KC. The worldwide influence of IHOP-KC to encourage intimacy with God and intercession for Israel is simply a miracle. It all goes to point toward this global movement in the end times of alignment between Israel and the church to establish Yeshua's kingdom on earth.

This sweeping movement of revelation about Israel and intercession for Israel has miracle stories all over the world. In the 1990s, it spread through China and Korea. Now it is happening spontaneously in every continent, including Southeast Asia, Africa, and even the Arab nations. How great is the grace of God!

Questions for Reflection

1. What are the three main prerequisites for the second coming?
2. How is the gospel of the kingdom to be preached in all the world?
3. How does the Bride come to her fullness?
4. How does worldwide prayer in the church bring about revival in Israel?

8

Global Alignment

Why is it that God seems to be speaking to so many about this word, *alignment*? My friends Ariel Blumenthal and David Demian have spent many years building relationships with Christians in mainland China. After several years of prayer-praise-prophecy meetings, some of the leaders sensed there was more that they needed to learn about Israel, the end times, and the kingdom of God.

They asked me to come teach for several days. I wasn't sure exactly what was going to happen. On the first morning, my wife and I arrived to meet with the leaders before the conference. The first thing they said was, "Will you teach us about alignment?" I was somewhat shocked. (I learned a new word in Mandarin: *duoe'che*—alignment.)

> *To understand God's alignment, to be
> able to identify with one another, to have
> a sense of belonging to one another,
> we must enlarge our hearts.*

Over the years, different groups from South Pacific islands have come to Israel and said: "We have come from the farthest ends of the earth. God is bringing the gospel back to Jerusalem in order to get ready for the second coming of Yeshua. We have come here because we want to be in the correct order of the covenant. We want to be rightly aligned with you, our Messianic brothers and sisters in Israel."

One group actually traveled by boat to a small island which is the farthest coordinate point on the globe from Jerusalem. They brought two small, volcanic rocks from the island as a sign of global realignment.

> *Yeshua's feet will "touch down" on the*
> *Mount of Olives; He will march triumphantly*
> *into Jerusalem; He will sit in the seat*
> *of government in Jerusalem.*

On another occasion, some dear friends drove by jeep all the way from Western China to Jerusalem to affirm the vision of the "silk road" and "back to Jerusalem."

Everyone seems to be hearing from the Holy Spirit that the time has come to be in right alignment. May the Lord help us and guide us to do what He is asking!

As I was praying in preparation to teach at a church in the Dallas area, the Lord put this issue of alignment on my heart. I had prayed a lot and hadn't sensed anything in particular. Then I suddenly had a clear sense of the Lord saying this one word, *alignment*. I had an image or discernment of this alignment being like the snap or "click" of a chiropractic treatment. That word and that image seemed to say it all.

The New Covenant describes the community of faith as a "body." It is important for the health of the overall body that the backbone and neck be in right alignment. If even the slightest link in the vertebrae is out of line, there will be pain in all different parts of the body. If the spinal cord is not straight or even slightly rubbing against the wrong bone, then the body can be paralyzed. One click to straighten out the backbone can free the whole body to full movement without pain.

Biblical teaching about alignment is to help bring about a similar chiropractic click for the "body" of Christ.

Another picture of alignment is the plumb line. Amos had a vision in which a divine figure in human form (presumably Yeshua) appeared to him on a wall holding a plumb line. **"Behold the Lord was standing on a wall set by a plumb line and in His hand was a plumb line. And the Lord said to me, 'What do you see, Amos?' and I said, 'a plumb line.' And the Lord said, 'Behold, I am setting a plumb line in the**

midst of my people Israel'" **(Amos 7:7–8).**

A plumb line is a builder's tool to ensure a wall is built straight and upright. It is a string with a weight on the end. God sets spiritual and moral standards which He will not allow to be violated. The vertical line will not be changed. Either we conform to the plumb line, or we will be judged.

One aspect of alignment is identification. Dan Juster has taught that "the church has been joined to Israel for the sake of world redemption. Israel is part of the identity of the church, and the church is part of the identity of Israel." Together they are the One New Man.

A change of identity is occurring in the international church and in the Messianic remnant. The change is a switch from "them" to "us." It is not "you" but "we." It is a sense of belonging and being part of. This change of identity is to some degree a redefinition of the ecclesia (or returning to its original definition). The realignment is essentially a change of identity. It is the church and Israel identifying one with another.

I recall in the year 2000, right after the outbreak of the Second Intifada, the saying began to spread among Israeli political and media leaders: "It seems like our only friends in the world are those who call themselves 'evangelical Christians.'"

Over the recent decades, Israel has been the safest place in the Middle East for Arab Christians. In general, the Arab Christian community in Israel is becoming more and more of a loved and appreciated sector of Israel society, in a greater way than ever before.

The church was always meant to see itself as a spiritual extension of the people of Israel. The Messianic remnant was meant to see the international ecclesia as its "offspring" or "progeny." Can the church say, "I am part of Israel?" Can the Messianic remnant say of the church, "You are part of my extended family" and "I am part of you"? Can we all say we belong to one another and that we are part of the same spiritual family?

At the Homecoming Gathering in Jerusalem in 2014, the International Convention Center was filled to capacity. Some of the Arab and Jewish brothers came onto the main platform together. I led a time of repentance on behalf of the Messianic community toward the Arab Christian community. We honored them as our brothers. We confessed that we were "married" together by covenant faith in Yeshua.

The time of repentance was so deep it was somewhat embarrassing. Then David Demian called the Arab brothers to respond. He led them in a faith declaration according to the Book of Ruth: **"Your people will be my people, and Your God will be my God."** A feeling of covenantal bonding was formed. A profound repositioning was taking place.

Until that moment, I thought that the "Ruth" calling was a unique and unusual calling for those few Christians whom God had led to be connected to the people of Israel. To see so many Arab leaders making that commitment changed my viewpoint. If Arab Christians can do this, why can't all Christians?

I realized that the Ruth example was supposed to be the normative one, not the Orphah example (Ruth 1:14–15). *Orphah* means "to turn the back of the neck." That can't be right. Ruth is a model for the entire ecclesia community. Ruth is not to be the exception but the rule. That should be logically apparent. If Yeshua is both head of the church and King of Israel, then we are to be joined as one people by faith.

(That does not mean that people lose their ethnic identity—quite the opposite. Each ethnic group *affirms* the other, as we are mutually supportive. No one can help Jews to be "true Jews" like the Arabs, and no one can help Arabs to be "true Arabs" like the Jews. However, first we have to see ourselves as belonging to one another in one family. We have to identify with one another.)

To love someone means there is a place for that person in your heart. To allow someone else to come in means you have to enlarge your heart. To understand God's alignment, to be able to identify with one another, to have a sense of belonging to one another, we must enlarge our hearts. That may sound easy, but it is more difficult than it sounds.

"We treated you with largeness of heart. Your place in our hearts is not narrow; but in your hearts the place is narrow. Widen the place in your heart toward us" (II Corinthians 6:11–12; 7:2).

> ### *Every community of faith should see itself as rooted in God's biblical mandate from Jerusalem.*

It is not always easy to stretch. Sometimes we have painful histories, negative narratives, cultural differences, and offensive miscommunications that need to be overcome. To stretch our hearts takes effort, caring, responsibility, commitment, time, forgiving, listening, dialoguing, etc. To enlarge your heart is to have a circumcision of heart. That is the price to be aligned as one body.

One of the first groups to grasp the fullness of this alignment was our friends at Aglow International with Jane Hansen Hoyt. Jane had come to see us in Israel as she had done regularly with her board and a large tour group. My wife, Betty, and I went to meet with them along with some of our younger team members.

Not long before that Ari and Shira Sorko-Ram had talked to us about taking oversight for the Tel Aviv congregation, Tiferet Yeshua (a wonderful congregation they founded and pioneered, and where we had worked with them previously as their assistants). In order for us to take leadership responsibility for this new stage of the congregation, we asked our friends Ron and Elana Cantor to join us. Ron and Elana served as primary congregational leaders, with Betty and me serving as overseers.

With our responsibilities already at the Revive Israel training center, Ahavat Yeshua congregation in Jerusalem, and the Tikkun International network, we were feeling quite overwhelmed.

Our other ministry team members said that if we were to receive oversight of the Tel Aviv congregation, I needed a corresponding ordination to clarify the role. The only biblical way to define multi-congregational leadership is the role of an apostle. (I try never to use the term "apostle" as a title, but only when necessary to explain the function.)

I realized it was the correct thing to do in this case. Everyone agreed; the leadership laid hands on me and Betty for impartation of greater wisdom, anointing, and authority in this expanded role, overseeing several congregations and ministries.

When Betty and I arrived at the meeting with Aglow, quite frankly, we were worn out. I told Betty I wasn't sure we could go on, but we put one foot in front of the other and went to pray as usual before the meeting. The only message I received in my heart was concerning the sufferings of Christ—to call people to follow in Yeshua's footsteps as sacrificial lamb and suffering servant, according to Isaiah 53. I told Betty, "I don't think anyone will enjoy this message."

When we met with Jane and the international board before the meeting, they asked us how things were going. We told them about the congregations, the team, and the networking. They said, "That's very significant." We responded, "Well, it's only significant if you think it is."

Jane said, "We at Aglow want to be aligned with the Messianic, Spirit-filled, apostolic remnant that God is restoring in this time. We want your team to bless us and send us out." I was shocked. I said, "Jane, you have a huge ministry, and we have very little." She said that was not important. They wanted to be rightly aligned with God's plan for His kingdom. They saw this as an opportunity for the Aglow network to be rightly aligned with Yeshua.

Betty and I asked the international board members if they agreed. They unanimously and heartily said, "Yes." Alignment is a right relationship of recognizing one another's callings. It is not a subjugation to hierarchical submission (although any kind of mutual submission requires a submissive heart). We all submit to God's pattern, which allows for mutual blessing to flow from God to us, and from one to another.

Well, the Holy Spirit seemed to bless the message on the sufferings of Christ, the prayer time, the laying on of hands, and the "sending out." Our relationship and alignment with Aglow has always been one of love and mutual respect.

The Aglow leadership saw this as an opportunity to connect with Yeshua's kingdom strategy. Their response said something about them, not us. The Aglow leadership has a sensitive heart to prophetic alignment in the Holy Spirit. Being sent out from part of the Messianic remnant in Jerusalem was their positioning themselves for greater kingdom anointing.

At another meeting, we took the whole group to the overlook between the Mount of Olives and Mount Zion. I said, "Look to the left and to the right." Just a kilometer or two on one side is the Mount of Olives, and on the other side is Mount Zion. It all seems so close you can touch it.

Biblical prophecy says in the clearest terms that Yeshua will return physically to the Mount of Olives and then reign in a real government on earth from Mount Zion. So here is the question: Do we believe that? Yeshua's feet will "touch down" on the Mount of Olives; He will march triumphantly into Jerusalem; He will sit in the seat of government in Jerusalem. Do we believe it is actually going to happen?

This is a special perspective that a visit to Israel can provide: the "reality" of biblical prophecies. This is a challenging question: Are end times prophecies literal and physical, or only spiritual and figurative? That is a profound reorientation.

We are making a faith connection to Messiah Yeshua, His capital, His kingdom, and His strategy. Every community of faith should see itself as rooted in God's biblical mandate from Jerusalem.

In November 2016, with three thousand attendees at the Global Gathering in Jerusalem Arena, David Demian and I shared in a worshipful ceremony to welcome Yeshua back to Jerusalem. Together with brothers and sisters from around the world (and particular inspiration from our amazing brothers from the South Pacific Samoan Islands), we lifted up a large model of a golden-colored crown.

In the center were Jewish and Arab believers in Yeshua. We were cooperating to welcome Messiah back with cries of "Barukh Haba," blessed is He who comes (Matthew 23:39). There was such a sense of excitement and wonder as Arabs, Jews, and internationals united in the Holy City to crown Yeshua as King Messiah. In that beautiful moment I lifted up the crown as an act of worship, offering the crown to Yeshua our King.

A historic pathway or highway of relationships is being formed.

There has been a progression in understanding the connections and cooperation to come to a global alignment for Yeshua's kingdom. A historic pathway or highway of relationships is being formed.

It starts with the Western church praying to be "one" according to John 17 and being the "one new man" according to Ephesians 2:11–15. Then it reaches to the Pacific Islands at the "ends of the earth" according to Acts 1:8 and Isaiah 49:6. After that, it embraces the "back to Jerusalem" movement of East Asia (Acts 16:6; Matthew 2:1; Isaiah 59:19) This connects to the Abrahamic family or "Isaiah 19 highway." (More about "back to Jerusalem" in chapter 10 and the "Isaiah 19 highway" in chapter 16.)

All these regions link as well to the Messianic community in Israel for the Barukh Haba invitation for Yeshua to return (Matthew 23:39). We had just a little taste of these connections becoming lined up. Let's summarize some of the "geographic" stages of this alignment as follows:

1. **One New Man:** Jew and Gentile—International Church—Ephesians 2:15
2. **Canoe Vision:** Ends of the Earth—Pacific Islands—Acts 1:8
3. **Silk Road:** Back to Jerusalem—East Asia—Acts 16:6
4. **Isaiah 19 Highway:** Abrahamic Family—Middle East—Isaiah 19:23
5. **Barukh Haba:** Messianic Remnant—Israel—Matthew 23:39

These all fit together in a perfect picture puzzle. On that evening in the Jerusalem Arena, representatives of this alignment were in place. The pieces were beginning to be connected. We could feel the presence of God in the stadium. Together we lifted up the crown of Yeshua to invite Him to be our king.

(Interesting Note: The gathering "happened" to be at the same time as the 2016 American presidential election. There was a huge outpouring of intercession on the night before the election for God's will to be done. It felt like a tidal wave of spiritual power and united prayer was released from Jerusalem toward the United States

We do not have any political aspirations. We intercede for the kingdom of God and His righteousness to come. The agenda is Yeshua, the power of the Holy Spirit, and setting His body in right covenantal order. The issue is getting ready and being prepared for what lies ahead of us.)

Questions for Reflection

1. What is the significance of the Pacific Islands in completing the Great Commission?
2. How does a chiropractic "click" affect the body?
3. What is the purpose of a plumb line?
4. How do the church and Israel identify with one another?
5. What are the five major geographic stages to global alignment?

9

Prerequisites for Second Pentecost

I am convinced that the right global alignment will lead to a worldwide revival in the end times. I referred to this almost forty years ago as "second Pentecost." Others have referred to it as the "Acts 2:17" vision.

> **This is what was spoken of by Yoel the prophet: In the last days…I will pour out My Spirit on all flesh, and your sons and daughters will prophesy; your young men will see visions; and your old men will dream dreams. And upon My servants and My maidservants I will pour out My Spirit in those days and they will prophesy…before the coming of the great and terrible day of YHVH. All those who call on the name of YHVH will escape.**
>
> **—Acts 2:16–19, 21**

Here Peter quotes the prophet Yoel (Joel) as part of his explanation to the crowd on the morning of Shavuot (Pentecost) immediately after the outpouring of the Holy Spirit in power, fire, and speaking in tongues.

> *I am convinced that the right global alignment will lead to a worldwide revival in the end times.*

When I say "second Pentecost," I mean that there is a future fulfillment to this prophecy, greater in numbers than what happened two thousand years ago. The past fulfillment was a single event that happened in Jerusalem. Today, any group of people can receive the power of the Holy

> *As the Messianic Jewish remnant*
> *is restored to the global ecclesia, we will*
> *all be more aligned for the "outpouring on*
> *all flesh" in the end times.*

Spirit at any time and any place.

The future fulfillment is not localized but international. It takes place not right after the first coming but right *before* the second coming. The Spirit is poured out on all flesh. The revival ushers in the second coming. Let's look at what must take place for this outpouring to be released.

In addition to the many universal elements of unity, maturity, and purity within the international ecclesia, here are seven specific prerequisites of alignment with Israel, set by God, that are necessary for the second Pentecost to take place:

1. Restoration of Israel
2. Restoration of the Messianic remnant within Israel
3. Restoration of five-fold ministry gifts within the Israeli remnant
4. Right relationship between Messianic Jews and the international church
5. Understanding of the end times
6. Understanding of the feasts of Israel
7. United prayer.

(Again, when I say "prerequisites," I do not mean that God is dependent on us, but that we must submit to and cooperate with the conditions He has set in Scripture for these events to take place.)

Why do I mention these particular elements which connect the future "Pentecost" to events in Israel? The first outpouring took place in Israel alone. The second one will be international yet still have Israel as its center. Yeshua came the first time to Jerusalem, and there also He will come the second time. Therefore, the outpouring must be connected to the same location.

Peter ends his quote from Joel in the middle of a verse. Let's look at the continuance:

> **...for in Mount Zion and in Jerusalem there will be a remnant...among the survivors whom YHVH has called. For in those days and at that time in which I will restore the captivity of Judah and Jerusalem...I will gather all the Gentile nations and bring them down to the valley of Jehoshaphat and will judge them there...**
>
> **—Joel 2:32–3:2**

I believe Peter did not quote this second half of the passage because it was not the time then (in the first century) for the worldwide outpouring to take place. However, it would seem apparent that Peter and the other disciples had been discussing and praying about Joel's prophecy.

"Because of the Remnant"

Notice the word *for* in verse 32 (*ki*, כי in Hebrew). The greater outpouring will take place "for" or "because" of something that will take place in Jerusalem. The reason behind the word *because* is what demands the alignment we are talking about.

Joel speaks of a remnant whom the Lord calls. I understand that as the Messianic remnant of faith. It is parallel to the group of Yeshua's early disciples.

That group is called out of a larger group called the "survivors." I understand the larger group to be all those Jews who have survived the wars, particularly the Holocaust and the coming wars of the end times. From the generation of those survivors, there will emerge a Messianic remnant "whom the Lord has called."

This remnant will be found after the "survivors" and during the "restoration" of the captivity of Judah. This is partly what the disciples were referring to when they asked Yeshua if He would restore the kingdom to Israel at that time. Compare:

– Acts 1:6—Will you at this time restore the kingdom to Israel?

– Joel 3:1—At that time when I restore the captivity of Judah...

There is a pre-set time for the restoration of the nation of Israel. Within the nation of Israel comes the restoration of the Messianic remnant as well.

That remnant is connected to all those among the nations who receive the Holy Spirit. That connection leads to the worldwide revival.

Restoring the Twelfth Apostle

Within the Messianic remnant, there must also be a restoration of apostles and prophets. I do not mean a restoration of the original twelve apostles of the Lamb, nor of the Israelite prophets who wrote the Tanakh (Law and Prophets). We mean apostles and prophets with a small "a" and "p," not the Apostles and—with a capital "A" or "P." However, just as there is a restoration of apostles, prophets, evangelists, pastors, and teachers in *every* nation (Ephesians 4:11–16), so must there *also* be in the Messianic remnant.

What took place in Acts 1 right before the outpouring in Acts 2?

The first half of Acts 1 describes Yeshua's giving the Great Commission of world evangelism and also His ascension into heaven. Acts 1:14 speaks of the community of disciples meeting regularly for united prayer. (More on that later.) Yet there is another factor here.

The second half of Acts 1, from verse 15 to 26, has to do with choosing the twelfth apostle who would replace Judas. If the number twelve was not important, they would not have replaced him. The apostolic mission of Yeshua's disciples was seen as being aligned with the pattern of the ancient tribes of Israel.

If there is to be another outpouring, there must be some restoration of apostolic-type ministry, both within Israel and around the world. This is a controversial and yet weighty issue. I have given much of my life to serve the restoration of apostolic and prophetic ministry in the Messianic remnant.

I began by serving on the team under Dan Juster in 1984. Dan led us to work with several other apostles and their networks among our Christian friends. Upon moving to Israel, I served for many years under Joe Shulam at Netivyah, then under Ilan Zamir at the Messianic Alliance, and then under Ari Sorko-Ram at Tiferet Yeshua. These all had apostolic, breakthrough pioneering ministries.

I consider many other wonderful men and women of God (too many to name here), both in Israel and the diaspora, to have served as apostles and prophets, even though most of them would prefer not to use the term. There are young people around the world today who have the potential and calling to be apostles and prophets. We are not trying to glorify any person. We are looking to reestablish important, normative, scriptural functions in the community of faith worldwide (Ephesians 2:22; 4:11).

Replacing Judas

There is also here a delicate issue of the replacement of Judas. In Hebrew, there is no difference between the names Judas or Jew or Judah. It is all *Yehuda* יהודה. Prophetic restoration in any people group often involves repenting of the "sins of our fathers" (Daniel 9:16; Exodus 20:5).

Among the sins of our people, which are many, is included the sin of betraying Yeshua. That sin, by Judas and our religious leaders (Matthew 26:21; 27:25), represents a deeply rooted spiritual curse and stumbling block that has been the source of horrible disasters for our people for two thousand years.

We as Messianic Jews seek to nullify and reverse that curse. As the crowd in the courtyard at the crucifixion of Yeshua cried, "Let his blood be upon us and upon our children" for a curse, we change that cry to "Let the blood of the Lamb of God be upon us and our children for redemption."

The reversal of that curse of betrayal into the blessing of the covenant starts a nuclear-type chain reaction of spiritual power. Such public confession and declaration releases freedom and blessing for revival and restoration. Whenever we have done this, the presence of the Holy Spirit has been tangible in our midst.

"To take part in this ministry and apostleship from which Judas by transgression fell…" (Acts 1:25).

It seems to me that to restore the apostolic position of Judas, we need to repent of the apostolic sin of Judas. (We are not talking about the perverted accusations of "Deicide" that have been used for demonic anti-Semitism and attempted genocide against our people. We are talking about biblical repentance of national sins in a way that our forefathers did.)

As the twelfth position of Judas had to be replaced in Acts 1 before the outpouring in Acts 2, the sense of my heart is that the Messianic Jewish remnant is symbolic of that "twelfth" position, in relationship to the other parts of international body. As the Messianic Jewish remnant is restored to the global ecclesia, we will all be more aligned for the "outpouring on all flesh" in the end times.

The spiritual outpouring at Pentecost was a one-time event in the year AD 33. It is also a continuing series of events that have happened around the world during the entire time since AD 33 (particularly worth mentioning are the Azusa Street revival in 1906 in California and the Jesus People movement starting in 1967).

The Pentecostal outpouring has past, present, and future dimensions. I believe that these outpourings will culminate in a final outpouring leading up to the second coming.

The 120 and the 3,000

When the Holy Spirit was poured out in Acts 2, we find an interesting interaction between two groups of people.

In Jerusalem there were dwelling God-fearing Jews from every people under the heavens.

—Acts 2:5

The inner core was made up of 120 Hebrew-speaking, native-born Israeli Galilean Jews. Surrounding them was a larger group of thousands of Torah-observant Jews and converts from many different nations, who all spoke different languages, coming to Jerusalem to celebrate the feast. This group later served as a bridge between the Israeli core and the many nations around the world from which they had come to worship in Jerusalem.

It was essential for these two groups to be in place. The outpouring had to take place during the feast. It had to take place in Jerusalem. There had to be a core of Israeli believers. There had to be a larger group of diaspora Jews. Around the diaspora Jews, there had to be people from many different nations. After the feasts, most of these "pilgrim" Jews and converts returned to their homes. Through them the gospel spread quickly around the world.

Those two groups of people set a pattern for the right relationship between Israel and the nations. There are circles within circles. Every person has his or her place. Everyone is equal. The alignment has to be in position so that no one will be missed. The alignment is designed to guarantee that everyone is included.

Religious prejudice seeks to exclude people by ethnic pride; covenantal alignment seeks to include everyone by preferring one another in honor (Romans 12:10).

Global alignment is the right relationship between the international ecclesia and the Israeli remnant. That puts everyone in position to receive the outpouring of the Holy Spirit.

A fascinating subset of that alignment is the relationship between the Israeli Messianic remnant and the diaspora Messianic remnant. The end-times Messianic Jewish remnant is found both in Israel and in the diaspora.

This is a fundamental issue that created challenges, even in the first-century community of faith. There were difficulties between the Greek-speaking Jews and the Hebrew-speaking Jews in the Jerusalem congregation (Acts 6:1–3). The issues had to do with communication, authority, budgeting, and so on.

It is amazing that the linguistic, cultural, and ethnic differences in the new community of faith caused so many challenges. We experience similar challenges today in our congregations. I imagine there are parallel issues in almost every country.

"Hurrying to Pentecost"—Future Prophetic Meaning

Since this great outpouring will lead up to the "Great and Terrible Day of YHVH," according to Joel and Peter, a basic understanding of end times prophecies will be a necessary component in global alignment.

Since the outpouring took place on the Feast of Shavuot, it will also be necessary to have a basic understanding of the symbolic and prophetic meaning of the feasts.

The question arises whether there is any future meaning to the Feast of Shavuot. All of the feasts have some dimension of prophetic and revelatory meaning. Since Acts 2:17 promises a future and greater outpouring of the

> ## *The Pentecostal outpouring has past, present, and future dimensions.*

Holy Spirit, the Feast of Shavuot has a symbolic purpose in reminding us to pray for spiritual outpouring.

Apparently, the apostle Paul (Shaul) felt the same way: **"Paul was hurrying on his way, in order that he might perhaps be able to be in Jerusalem for the feast of Shavuot [Pentecost]" (Acts 20:16).**

Paul was hurrying; therefore, he must have thought that being in Jerusalem for this feast had some importance. (See also I Corinthians 16:8.)

This journey took place long after the Acts 2 Pentecost; therefore, Paul must have thought there was a continuing significance of the feast, as looking to the future.

He was trying to get to Jerusalem; therefore, he must have thought that continuing prayer on the day of Shavuot would be part of preparing the way for the great end times revival. (The location of Jerusalem, the meaning of the feasts, end-times prophecies, Jew and Gentile reconciliation, and intercessory prayer all become significant.)

If it was urgent for Paul to pray in Jerusalem during Shavuot-Pentecost, so should prayer on that day be significant to us.

United Prayer

And this leads us to the last point of alignment: united prayer. United prayer leads to revival. This united prayer is one of the reasons we are committed to our dear friends at Global Gathering, at The Call, and at IHOP-KC. Their prayers and those of many others are changing the world.

> **All these continued in one heart in prayer.**
>
> **—Acts 1:14**

In the first great outpouring of the Holy Spirit, there were 120 Galilean followers of Yeshua praying in unity leading up to the Feast of Pentecost. What would it take to release a worldwide outpouring?

United prayer leads to revival.

I believe we need the Messianic remnant in Israel praying together on Shavuot with multitudes of brothers and sisters from every nation around the world.

For years we have helped to organize all-day or all-night prayer events on Pentecost eve in order to intercede for the outpouring of the Holy Spirit in the end times. Today, because of the internet and social media and live streaming, the ability to join together in united worldwide prayer is almost unlimited. Who could have ever imagined such a thing?

The day of Pentecost reminds us of the event of Pentecost, which reminds us of the future worldwide Pentecostal revival. This is alignment. Cooperation in prayer between Messianic Jews, Arab Christians, and the international ecclesia on the Feast of Shavuot will be part of paving the way for a worldwide revival in the end times based on the pattern of Pentecost in Acts 2.

Let's do it!

Questions for Reflection

1. What does "second Pentecost" mean?
2. What is the second half of the prophecy in Joel that Peter did not quote in Acts 2?
3. Is there a purpose today to fulfilling the ministry and apostleship that Judas left?
4. Who were the two groups of people present at the "first Pentecost"?
5. How does unified prayer lead to revival?

10

Time and Geography

Time and geography are sometimes important in the kingdom of God, and sometimes not. In speaking to the Samaritan woman at the well, Yeshua said, **"The time is coming when not on this mountain and not in Jerusalem will you worship the Father. You worship what you do not know; we worship what we do know; for salvation is from the Jews. The time is coming and now is when true worshipers will worship the Father in spirit and in truth"** (John 4:21–23).

There is a time to worship in Jerusalem; there is a time not to worship in Jerusalem. In order to worship in spirit and truth, no association with geography or time is needed. To worship internationally, there is no need of any ethnic identity. Yet the acknowledgment that salvation comes from the Jews remains as a fact of divine covenant.

> *As we approach the return of Yeshua to planet earth, the time and the land become important again.*

For much of the international Christian world, there has been little importance to time and geography for the last two millennia. In the Jewish worldview, time and geography are of utmost importance. Geography is described in terms of *Jerusalem, Judea, Galilee,* and *diaspora.* Time is described by the calendar of Sabbaths, New Moons, and Holy Days.

God created the world both spirit and matter. To the spirit dimension, time and geography are irrelevant. To the material dimension, time and geography are essential. In the age of the Holy Spirit, time and geography are not stressed. As we approach the return of Yeshua to planet earth, the

> *The mystery of time and non-time, of geography and non-geography, is part of the mystery of Israel and the church, of Jew and Gentile.*

time and the land become important again.

When Yeshua was here, the spirit and the geography coincided. He was here in a body, and the Spirit was in Him. After He ascended, He was not on earth, yet the Holy Spirit was poured out. For the initial outpouring, the location was essential. Later on, geographical restrictions were totally removed. (That is one reason why the spread of the gospel coincided with the destruction of Jerusalem and the dispersion of the Jewish people.) Ultimately, spirit and geography will be united again.

[Note two Hebrew words in Genesis chapter 1: appointed time is *mo'ad* מוֹעֵד. Genesis 1:14 says that the stars and moon were given for appointed times. The appointed times in Leviticus 23 are also the Holy Days. The Holy Days are connected to the stars, which are part of God's creation. God's pre-destined time schedule is built into the creation. The Holy Days and the stars are coordinated with God's pre-destined plan.

The second Hebrew word of note here is, meaning to rule or govern, is *memshelah,* מֶמְשָׁלָה. Genesis 1:16 says that the sun rules the day, and the moon rules the night. That word for rule is used today for modern government. We may possibly see here in Genesis a symbolic hint that there are two levels of government in the kingdom of God: sun government and moon government. The "sun" government represents people who have been raised from the dead and glorified (I Corinthians 15:40–42). The "moon" government represents natural people ruling on earth. The glorified woman of Revelation 12:1 is clothed with the sun, and the moon is under her feet.

We don't want to exaggerate or read too much into the words *mo'ad* and *memshelah*. The point is simply that already in Genesis 1, we see a certain connection between the feasts of Israel, natural creation, heavenly bodies, spiritual authority, times, seasons, and the predestined plan of God.]

Yeshua gave a basic strategy to His disciples in Acts 1:5–8. They must stay in Jerusalem. They must wait for the outpouring of the Holy Spirit. Then they must leave Jerusalem. Jerusalem would be destroyed. They were not to know the time of its rebuilding.

Time is connected to Jerusalem. While Jerusalem is in place, the clock is ticking. When Jerusalem is destroyed, time seems to change dimensions until the time for restoration returns. Daniel studied the writings of Jeremiah to determine when the time was appointed to rebuild Jerusalem (Daniel 9:2). The mystery of time and non-time, of geography and non-geography, is part of the mystery of Israel and the church, of Jew and Gentile. Yeshua Himself is also "inside" the dimension of time and "outside" of time in different situations.

In Acts 1:8, the disciples were instructed to travel out from Jerusalem. Apparently, they didn't listen. In Acts 8:1 they were forced out by persecution. (Some have said that if you don't choose Acts 1:8, you get Acts 8:1.)

In the first century, the gospel had a clear direction: from Jerusalem to the ends of the earth. For the following two thousand years, there has been somewhat less emphasis on direction. In this last century, a strategic emphasis returns, and the direction reverses from the ends of the earth back to Jerusalem.

If you change geographic location, you have direction. When you travel in a certain direction, you have created a "vector." This is the vector of the kingdom: Jerusalem outward; then circling the world; then return to Jerusalem. In physics, there is centrifugal-fission power going outward and centripetal-fusion power coming inward. The heart sends blood outward through the arteries and pulls it back through the veins. The kingdom goes out and the kingdom comes in.

When Yeshua told His disciples that they were not to know the times set by the Father, He meant that it was not the time for the restoration of Jerusalem; therefore, there was no need for them to know. God certainly does want us to know the time and season we are living in at any point in history so that we can obey Him in our current season. When it comes time to obey, you will know what time it is and what to do.

In fact, Yeshua rebuked His disciples for "not" discerning the times and the seasons (Matthew 16:3). We are expected to know what the times and the seasons are (I Thessalonians 5:1). When Yeshua said that His coming would be as a thief in the night, He meant that so it would seem for those living in sin or spiritual darkness (verse 2).

Only if we do not repent will the time of judgment come as a surprise (Revelation 3:3). As sons of the light, we are to know the times: **"You brethren are not in darkness so that this Day should overtake you as a thief" (I Thessalonians 5:4).**

We are to have spiritual discernment about the times and seasons. There is a time for scattering stones and a time for gathering stones together (Ecclesiastes 3:5). Similarly, there are two general biblical paradigms for the times and seasons:

1. Times of the Gentiles, with exile of the Jews, scattering (Genesis 15:13; Luke 21:24; Romans 11:25)
2. Times of restoration, with a return to the Land, regathering (Daniel 9:24; Psalm 102:13; Acts 1:6; 3:21; Romans 11:15)

At the beginning of the Book of Acts, Yeshua's disciples were a group of Galileans staying in the land of Judah (Acts 1:11). On the morning of Pentecost, the Galilean group met a group of diaspora Jews who had come to the feast (Acts 2:5). Later the gospel began to reach the Samaritans (Acts 8:5), the Ethiopian official traveling in Israel (Acts 8:27), the Roman centurion in Caesarea (Acts 10:1), Cyprus, and Syria (Acts 11:19).

Notice the change in describing the geographic alignment. Jerusalem is omitted and Galilee is added:

"Jerusalem, all Judea and Samaria, unto the ends of the earth" (Acts 1:8).

"All Judea, and the Galilee and in Samaria" (Acts 9:31).

Then the gospel takes a leap forward by the church in Antioch (Acts 13:4–5). Antioch (Antakya) as well as all seven churches of the Book of Revelation (chapters 2–3), Galatia, and Tarsus are all in modern-day Turkey. Turkey was in some ways the first "Christian" nation, although at the

> ## *This is the vector of the kingdom: Jerusalem outward, then circling the world, then returning to Jerusalem.*

time they were part of the Greek empire.

It is ironic that Turkey dominated the Middle East for most of modern history until the twentieth century as a Muslim Caliphate called the Ottoman empire. The Ottomans conquered the Middle East, including Jerusalem, in the year 1517. They controlled it until 1917, when they were driven out by the British under General Allenby.

The British were a Protestant nation. The common narrative of Allenby's conquest of Jerusalem says that he approached the city riding a white horse. When he arrived at the gate to Jerusalem, he dismounted and said, "There is only One who has the right to enter this city on a white horse, and it's not me."

Another turning point in history also happened in 1517: Martin Luther posted his famous Ninety-five Theses that, in effect, caused the outbreak of the Protestant Reformation.

Jerusalem was recaptured by the Jewish people in 1967, exactly fifty years after the British conquest. The year 1967 also marks the year of the start of the modern Charismatic Renewal.

I wrote the first edition of this book in 2017. Earlier that year, then US President Donald Trump visited Israel, becoming the first US president in history to pray at the Temple Wall while in office. There were also major alignment gatherings planned with Lou Engle and the Call in New York, with David Demian and the Egyptian church, and with Avi Mizrachi and Pacific Island leaders in Jerusalem.

The year 2017 marked a "speed up" in the global alignment pattern. There was a shift in seasons, an opening of a seal of understanding the Scriptures on these issues.

This book is being republished in 2023, the fiftieth-year anniversary from the Yom Kippur (Day of Atonement) war in 1973, which was perhaps the most significant and disastrous turning point so far in the history of modern Israel.

Let us recall that a period of fifty years is somewhat symbolic in Scriptures and is called a Jubilee. No one knows the exact dates of the original biblical Jubilee years. In any case, it is fascinating to notice this passage of time:

- 1517: Ottoman empire conquers Jerusalem
- 1517: Beginning of Luther's Protestant Reformation
- 1917: British Protestants conquer Jerusalem
- 1967: Jewish nation conquers Jerusalem
- 1967: Charismatic Renewal
- 2017: Global alignment pattern.

Let's summarize these years from 2017:

- 1517 was five hundred years before or ten Jubilees.
- 1917 was one hundred years before or two Jubilees.
- 1967 was fifty years before or one Jubilee.

Israel became a nation in 1948. The year 2018 was seventy years from that time. A period of seventy years is described as turning point dates for the restoration of the kingdom to Israel (Jeremiah 25:11; 29:10; Daniel 9:2, 24). The period of seventy years is to cross over to a new paradigm from what happened previously. It is to cross into the next historic stage.

The year 2018 was a seventy-year completion for the State of Israel. Now is the time for the next stage. It is the time for the spiritual restoration to rise out of the natural restoration. It is the time for the revival stage of the restoration of the nation of Israel. It is the time for the Messianic remnant of Israel to take its place.

(I do NOT AT ALL think we should overemphasize dates, but it is indeed worth having a bit of historical perspective for the times we live in.)

In Acts 16 there is another significant change in the time/geography vector of the gospel. Paul arrives in Turkey and is planning to turn eastward toward Asia. In an unusual revelation, the "Spirit of Yeshua" did not allow him to go in that direction (Acts 16:7). The next night Paul received a dream about a Macedonian (Greek) man beckoning him to come (verse 9). At that moment Paul made a strategic decision that changed all of history.

Paul understood that God was calling him to travel westward into Europe (verse 10). The decision for Paul to move westward instead of eastward marked a historic change in the direction of the kingdom of God for the next two thousand years. It established a certain "time and geography" pattern for world missions in the "ecclesia age."

After Paul's ministry time in Greece, he eventually wound up in Rome. In retrospect, this was the obviously correct decision since Rome was the capital of the empire that ruled the world.

The known world was dominated by Greek culture in the years before Yeshua's birth and dominated by Roman government in the years after His birth. Some scholars have credited the positive development of Greek philosophy and Roman government to be an indication of a divine hand guiding the spread of early Christianity into Europe.

In any case, the spread of the gospel did go westward in a general sense (although there were, of course, significant missions in many other nations and directions). The westward movement seemed to continue over the centuries into Western Europe and eventually into America and, finally, across the Pacific into East Asia.

This pattern is seen as significant by many East Asian Christians. Our generation has seen great revival in South Korea and in China. Almost all estimates agree that over one hundred million people have come to faith in Yeshua.

Many of the Far East Christians interpret this phenomenon to be proof of the "back to Jerusalem" or "road to Jerusalem" destiny. The main idea is that God has chosen the East Asian peoples to lead the spread of the gospel in this generation, continuing westward across Asia and the Muslim peoples until arriving back in the Middle East in preparation for the second coming of Yeshua.

The idea that the gospel of the kingdom will return to Israel "from the

| *We are to have spiritual discernment about the times and seasons.* |

east" loops us back in thought all the way to the birth of Yeshua. There we saw **"wise men from the East" (Matthew 2:1)**. They brought prophecy about the Messiah to Israel before the people of Israel realized that the prophecy was about to be fulfilled.

The revelation about Messiah may have been spread throughout the East in the time of Daniel, Mordechai, and Ezekiel in the Eastern diaspora of Persia and Babylon. It may have come before that, at the time that the sons of Abraham through Keturah were sent out to the East (Genesis 25:6). And it may have its origin even before that, when Adam was sent out of Eden to the East, and Abraham as the son of Noah coming back from the East toward the land of Canaan.

In any case, the westward direction coming from the East and ending up back from the East seems to be an early biblical pattern that was later reemphasized by the Holy Spirit to Paul in Acts 16:6. There is also a mention of the East prophetically in Isaiah 41:25; 59:19 and Revelation 7:2. It is exciting for the peoples of the Far East to see a biblically pre-destined plan for what is taking place in their countries in this generation. It is a demonstration of the sovereignty of God.

In addition, the massive number of people who live in Asia, East Asia, Southeast Asia, and the Indian subcontinent tips the scales of balance as we look at the overall picture of the kingdom of God and the body of Christ in our generation.

The fact that millions of Christians all across East Asia and Southeast Asia see themselves as part of God's plan to bring the gospel from the Far East back to Jerusalem is a historic paradigm shift, catapulting global alignment strategy into a whole new dimension.

In the 1940s some of the Chinese Christians actually began a pilgrimage westward to share the gospel across Asia to return back to Jerusalem. They were arrested and persecuted. Just as I finished editing this chapter,

I received word that the last pioneer of that movement, a dear pastor in his nineties who had spent over twenty years in jail, went on to be with the Lord.

Right before he died, another pastor visited him at his bedside and shared with him that millions of Chinese had come to faith, that the gospel was spreading through the Middle East, and that there were even Jewish believers in Israel today. I saw the video clip of him hearing these words and smiling as a heavenly peace and light seemed to spread across his face.

Questions for Reflection

1. Why is time and geography less important in the "church" age?
2. Why is time and geography more important as we approach the second coming?
3. Are we to know the times and seasons or not to know them (Matthew 16:3; I Thessalonians 5:1–4; Revelation 3:3)?
4. What two significant events took place in 1517?
5. How is the revelation to Paul in Acts 16:7 significant to Christians in East Asia?

11

The Jerusalem Council

Cooperation with God's plans always involves submission to authority. The first kind of authority is directly to God in spirit. However, submission is also secondarily to delegated authority through men and women in positions appointed by God.

The New Covenant ecclesia is by its very nature a community with delegated spiritual authority. The highest level of authority in the Torah was Moses; the highest in the Israelite kingdom was David. In the New Covenant, there is a change of structure. It is more flexible, relational, and led by the Holy Spirit; yet it is still clearly authoritative.

> *The entire group of leaders saw themselves as submitted to the Holy Spirit.*

The widest structure of authority in the New Covenant is found in the meeting between the apostolic leaders and Jerusalem elders, recorded in Acts 15. It is known as the Acts 15 Council or the Jerusalem Council. As it was such an inclusive level of authority, it also represents the ultimate pattern of alignment. At that time the international ecclesia alignment came to a certain "summit" meeting at the Jerusalem Council.

The council takes place quite a few years after the Acts 2 revival. Paul said in Galatians 1 that he had not seen the apostles in Jerusalem for three years (verse 18). Then he said after another fourteen years he went up to Jerusalem for a "special meeting" (Galatians 2:1–2). It seems likely that this was the same meeting described in Acts 15. This would place the timing of the meeting approximately twenty-five years after the Pentecost revival.

Paul speaks of Barnabas as a coworker and Titus as a staff member (Galatians 2:1). Apparently, part of the discussion in Acts 15 about circum-

Cooperation with God's plans always involves submission to authority.

cision had to do with Titus as a specific example (Galatians 2:3). Paul also mentions that John was present at the meeting (Galatians 2:9) although John is not mentioned in Acts 15.

The context of the Jerusalem Council is probably also given in Galatians 2, which describes the confrontation between Peter and Paul at Antioch (verse 11) and even the initial disagreement with Barnabas (verse 13). These disagreements showed the necessity for a meeting of the senior leaders to give direction.

Congregations had been established all over the Middle East: Turkey, Greece, Egypt, Ethiopia, Cyprus, Syria, and Israel. It was just beginning to become clear that the ministry of the apostle Paul was at the forefront of the gospel mission. Yet his vision about the growth of the international church and the role of the Gentiles was still quite controversial.

Although Paul had at that point still the lowest level of position among the other apostles, his influence, leadership, and vision ended up being recognized by everyone there. He was the dominating figure because of the fruit of his work and the anointing of the Holy Spirit on what he had to say. His authority here was influential more than positional.

The controversy about the growth of faith among the Gentiles led to the assembling of leaders to Jerusalem to discuss the issues. This council represents the only example in the New Covenant of convening senior inter-congregational leadership and, therefore, has much to instruct us about ecclesia government and alignment.

Let's look at the pattern of the Acts 15 Council in three dimensions:

1. Structure of the meeting

2. Process of decision making

3. Content of the topics discussed.

The very existence of the Jerusalem Council demonstrates that the congregations of faith around the whole world recognized the spiritual authority of senior leaders called "apostles and elders" (Acts 15:2), or "apostles and prophets" (Ephesians 2:20), or "apostles, prophets, evangelists, pastors and teachers" (Ephesians 4:11).

The role of apostles and prophets was not seen as a "roof" of government that was imposed upon them from above; rather it was seen as a foundation of faith and vision upon which the congregations were built. New Covenant spiritual authority is "bottom-up" in the sense that the leadership serves and lays foundations for others to be built up. The ecclesia was: **"built upon the foundation of the apostles and prophets; with Messiah Yeshua Himself as the chief cornerstone" (Ephesians 2:20).**

Modern New Covenant apostles and prophets do not lay *the* foundation of the body of Messiah. That was done by Yeshua and the Twelve. Yet we can take by inference, that they help to establish guidelines, vision, and structure for starting new local congregations today. One of the primary functions of "five-fold" Ephesians 4 type ministry teams is to encourage the multiplication and strengthening of local congregations of faith.

An apostolic team should build, train, support, and cause growth. It also has a role to oversee and govern. This team is composed of **"apostles, prophets, evangelists, pastors and teachers" (Ephesians 4:11;** see also **I Corinthians 12:28).** This is a pattern we see throughout the Book of Acts and the epistles.

1. **Salvation and Lordship**—Every believer in Yeshua saw himself as committed and submitted to follow Yeshua and obey the leading of the Holy Spirit (Romans 10:9).

2. **Congregational Membership**—Every believer joined a local congregation, which in turn, was part of the universal ecclesia. No one would have considered himself to be a believer and not part of a community (Matthew 16:18, Acts 2:41, 47; 4:32; 16:5).

3. **Eldership Authority**—Every congregation had elders who were appointed and ordained. There were clear standards of character and trustworthiness for a person to be chosen for eldership (Acts 14:23, I Timothy 3:1–7, Titus 1:5).

4. **Apostolic Leadership**—All of the congregational leadership accepted the authority of the apostles who laid the foundation for

the congregation. There was not one congregation recorded in the New Covenant that did not accept apostolic oversight.

5. **Senior Council**—The senior apostolic leaders would meet from time to time in a mutually submissive environment to hold one another accountable and to discuss foundational theological issues (Acts 15, Galatians 2:2).

Paul wrote to Titus, who by this time had become his assistant apostle: **"I left you in Crete to set in order what still needs to be set in order, and to appoint elders in every city, as I have commanded you" (Titus 1:5).** Notice here the word "every." Every believer was part of a congregation; every congregation had elders; every congregation recognized apostolic authority. There was no alternative. Although the submission to spiritual authority was voluntary, the authority was clearly accepted.

Through the senior apostles, every congregation saw itself as connected to Israel. The congregations were an extension of the ministry of the apostles. The apostles were rooted in Israel. The apostles were seen as the carriers of the prophetic vision of Israel. Every congregation was part of the greater Israelite "commonwealth" (Ephesians 2:12). Every New Covenant congregation had that spiritual link to Israel.

The ecclesia identified itself as part of the Israelite Messianic kingdom, now being spread to the nations. Because of the connection through the apostles, there was no Gentile congregation in the New Covenant period that did not see itself as connected to Israel.

So many Gentiles became believers in Yeshua that it was not clear to what extent they were to be part of Judaism or the Jewish people. The explosive growth of the new congregations demanded new guidelines about how to live. The pressure of some of the Jerusalemite believers to make the Gentiles become Jews and observe Jewish religious traditions was becoming oppressive. This was the issue that caused the Jerusalem Council to be convened.

The apostles and elders met to investigate the matter. After a long argument, Peter stood up and said, "Men and brothers..."

—Acts 15:6–7

> *Because of the connection through the*
> *apostles, there was no Gentile congregation*
> *in the New Covenant period that did not*
> *see itself as connected to Israel.*

There was a brotherly environment and mutual respect for the different leaders. The differences of opinion were great, even harsh. They spent much time giving each of the senior leaders a chance to speak. They argued. They discussed. They listened. They prayed.

There seemed to be five key leaders involved who had the most influence: Peter, John, James (the brother of Yeshua), Paul, and Barnabas. These leaders demonstrated mutual submission one to another (at least when they weren't arguing ☺).

I used to think that Jacob (James) was the head or "president" of the organization. That comes from the fact that after the discussion and prayer, Jacob makes the final decision, "Therefore I set judgment..." (Acts 15:19). There is no doubt that Jacob played a key role. He was the leader of the Jerusalem congregation. He was also the brother of Yeshua. (There also was some recognition of his royal descent from King David that reinforced his position.)

However, as we look at the whole passage, Peter was also given a primary place in leading the discussion. What is more convincing is that the final decision went in the direction that Paul led, as the new visionary with the correct "God-ordained" paradigm shift. The spiritual influence of the anointing on Paul set the direction for the group. The entire group of leaders saw themselves as submitted to the Holy Spirit. They had an organizational structure, but that structure was secondary to leading and presence of the Holy Spirit.

The way they addressed one another ["brothers" (verse 6), "beloved" (verse 25)] demonstrated how much mutual submission and godly respect they had for one another.

The decision was made through prayer and listening to the leading of the Holy Spirit. **"It seemed good to the Holy Spirit and to us..." (Acts 15:28).** The method of coming to a decision here is crucial because it determines the alignment and the authority. The decision-making process had three components:

1. Group discussion (verse 6)
2. Management decision (verse 19)
3. Prayer discernment (verse 28)

If any one of these elements is missing, the direction will go askew. There is a balance between the spiritual, the democratic, and the organizational. There was organizational hierarchy, but it was only one-third of the weight of influence in making the decisions.

Here is the issue: When we come to the highest level of ecclesia authority, do we arrive at one person as the representative of Christ on earth, or do we see a group of mutually submitted senior leaders who pray and discuss issues together? I believe the second option is more accurate biblically.

Each of these leaders was a senior apostle and had clear vertical authority in all the congregations they were supervising. However, when it came to the senior apostolic fathers meeting together to deal with issues that affected various apostolic streams together, the council members demonstrated mutual submission. There is a team leader, but there is recognition of separate spheres of authority at the same time. There is a delicate and organic balance between hierarchical leadership and mutual submission.

Over the years at Tikkun Global we maintained a group of senior overseers. (Dan Juster, Eitan Shishkoff, Michael Brown, Paul Wilbur, Don Finto, and David Rudolph have been part of that leadership at various times.) For four decades, we have met annually to discuss common issues relating to all of us.

Issues within one leader's sphere are usually not raised. We talk and pray about issues that cross streams or overlap spheres. Some of the issues brought up on this level are:

1. Mutual accountability and counseling
2. Ordination of senior leaders
3. Arbitration of problems between leaders
4. Foundational theological questions
5. Strategies for cooperation.

We look to the Acts 15 Council as a biblical example and pattern of how senior leaders can meet and submit one to another. We are not claiming to be *the* Jerusalem Council. In fact, I don't think it is numerically feasible or advisable to convene a one-world council. What was the *one* example of Acts 15 serves as the pattern for *many* in various settings today. (Symbolically the one menorah lampstand of the Tabernacle became many different lampstands in the Book of Revelation [1:13, 20].)

We are saying that senior leaders should meet at least once a year for mutual relationships, commitment, and accountability. Many denominations and new-stream charismatic churches follow this pattern of decision making. (Note today growing unity organizations in the Evangelical, Pentecostal, and Charismatic associations.)

I once knew a group of five of the senior leaders of mega churches in Seoul, Korea. Each of the five had a home church of over twenty-five thousand members with many satellite churches connected to them. "The Five" would go away periodically for a time of personal relationships, accountability, and discussions. I asked one of them to tell me what type of topics they discussed as senior leaders. He said their most common topic was "finishing well."

The testimony that we have at Tikkun Global of forty years of leaders walking in covenant, cooperation, and mutual accountability provides a basis for trust, safety, and stability that has been a blessing to many. We are just one of many streams, but we seek to pattern our senior leadership after the model of Acts 15, as many others have as well.

Right government and alignment in the New Covenant is that the senior leaders will meet periodically in an atmosphere of mutual submission and accountability. A mutually submitted team of senior leaders is our highest level of inter-congregational structure.

Out of the Jerusalem Council came a simple written statement which was sent to many congregations around the world. The unity of direction and clarity of the written decision caused growth among all of the congregations (Acts 16:4–5).

Many dear friends, such as Marty Waldman, Dan Juster, Benjamin

| *There is a delicate and organic balance between hierarchical leadership and mutual submission.* |

Berger, John Dawson and others, have been involved in "Toward Jerusalem Council II," which seeks to bring senior church leaders into a recognition of God's plan for Israel and a commitment to right ecclesiological government.

From time to time, as a result of their consultation meetings, they print pamphlets describing policy and theological statements. Like many other groups around the world, they are also seeking to follow the biblical pattern of the Acts 15 Council.

It is worth examining not only the structure of the Jerusalem Council but the content of the issues they were dealing with. It seems to me that the Jerusalem Council dealt with three primary topics, which amazingly enough are still three very key topics facing us today in the gatherings of multiple church streams:

1. Spheres of congregational authority

2. Jew and Gentile relationships

3. Balance of Law and grace.

(How did they deal with those issues? How are we to deal with those same issues today?)

Immediately after the council, Paul and Barnabas chose to separate. They had been one team; then they became two. Paul was originally under Barnabas' oversight. However, Paul was bringing a new paradigm from the Lord in a greater dimension of apostolic authority. God was creating a new sphere or "kanon" (II Corinthians 10:13) to reach the nations.

We have learned that there needs to be enough "room" for each person to operate in his own gifts. I call this "enough space to swing the bat" (to use a baseball analogy). In recognizing one another's callings, we need to make enough room for one another to succeed. New stages of leadership can sometimes make for difficult transitions.

Sometimes those transitions are painful, as apparently was the case with Paul and Barnabas (Acts 15:39). My personal sense is that the issue at hand was not so much the decision about John Mark, but about who was to be the leader. Barnabas had been Paul's leader, and now it was clear that there was an anointing and authority on Paul.

There was a change of leadership which demanded a change in spheres of authority. I wonder, had they discussed this first with James, John, and Peter, if they could have created two teams with less tension and argument.

Questions for Reflection

1. How does the conflict between Peter and Paul in Galatians 2 form the background to the Jerusalem Council in Acts 15?
2. Is there a purpose to apostolic leadership in the body of Messiah today?
3. How are the three elements of discernment, discussion and decision-making relevant to us today?
4. How should senior leaders submit one to another?
5. What were the three main topics discussed at the Acts 15 Council?

12

Ladder of Law and Grace

The issue of law and grace was a foundational issue at the Acts 15 council and is still relevant to the entire body of Christ today. We receive questions every day in Israel and around the world on how to stay balanced in the dynamic tension between law and grace. We do not want to fall into the extremes of "antinomianism" (anti-Law teaching) on the one side or religious legalism on the other.

Messianic Jews have done much good to help restore the proper place of the Torah (Law of Moses); yet at the same time, we have caused much confusion. I am quite sorry for all the misunderstandings. The subject is indeed complex. I would like to explain my position through a simple, five-rung ladder of priorities.

> *The issue of law and grace was a foundational issue at the Acts 15 Council and is still relevant to the entire body of Christ today.*

The word *law* is used in different ways in Scriptures and in Judaism and Christianity. Actually, the word **Torah** תורה does not mean "law" but "instruction." A teacher is *moreh*; a parent is *horeh*, instruction is *hora'ah*. The Torah is simply the first part of the Bible, the instruction of God. In Hebrew, there is not much difference between the words for Bible and the word for "law." God's word is His Law.

On the other hand, Torah has become a general name in Judaism for all rabbinic tradition and culture. Most Jews do not discern the difference between Jewish culture and biblical instruction. This confusion has caused huge damage to our own people. When that confusion passes over to our Gentile Christian friends, the result can be damaging and embarrassing.

Salvation by grace is the basic message of the gospel.

Here is the **Five-Step Ladder of Law and Grace**:

1. Salvation by Grace
2. Absolute Moral Law
3. Lighter Moral Law
4. Biblical Symbolism
5. Cultural Tradition.

A surprisingly large part of the Gospels and Epistles deals with the subject of Law and grace. Here is a brief summary of the five-rung ladder:

I. Salvation by Grace

Salvation by grace is the basic message of the gospel. Yeshua died on the cross as a substitute punishment so that we may receive forgiveness through believing in Him. He rose from the dead so that we may receive eternal life. When we submit to Yeshua as Lord, we pass from death to life. In that grace, every other blessing of God is also available.

We have sinned, yet God loves us. He is good and all-powerful. As we repent, He forgives. As we believe, we receive. He delights to give us all good things. Yeshua is the sum of all those good and excellent things.

This message of the grace of God is itself a kind of Torah. It is the "law" of spirit and life which overcomes the "law" of sin and death.

Romans 8:2—"The law of the spirit of life in Messiah Yeshua has set me free from the law of sin and death." If we ever lose sight of the gospel of grace, we have lost all the goodness which God so desires to give us.

Since we have no ability to rescue ourselves out of sin and death, any attempt to justify ourselves by keeping the law of our own strength is doomed. Self-righteousness misses the depth to which we have fallen and the need for the gracious intervention of God in our lives. Life is not about our being good; life is about God's goodness and love for us.

Romans 10:3–4—"Since they did not know the righteousness of God, and tried to establish their own righteousness, they did not sub-

mit to the righteousness of God. For the Messiah is the goal of the Law, in order that all who believe will be made righteous."

The word for "goal" here in Greek is *teleioo*, which is often translated as "perfection" or "completeness." The Messiah is the Law coming into its full perfection, not the doing away of moral standards.

The Law was not meant for us to achieve self-righteousness, but to make us aware of the holy standard of God and how we have sinned. That awareness makes us turn to Him in humble repentance and ask for His mercy.

Galatians 3:21, 24—"Is the Law contrary to the promises of God? God forbid! ... The Law is the schoolmaster directing us to the Messiah."

The Law, therefore, is the proper introduction to grace. The Law is the diagnosis; grace is the medicine. Yeshua is the doctor (Galatians 3:19–24).

II. Absolute Moral Law

God is Holy. He has given us moral law to show us where we violate His holiness. Anyone who believes in God must obey God's absolute moral law. The heart of the Law is simply to love God and love one another (Deuteronomy 6:5; Leviticus 19:18; Mark 12:29–31). A born-again person should have the Law written on his heart in such a way that he will want to obey God (Jeremiah 31:31–33).

In this way, there is no contradiction between Law and grace. Yeshua came to fulfill the Law, not abrogate it.

Matthew 5:17—"Do not think that I have come to nullify the Law and the Prophets; I did not come to nullify but to fulfill."

Yeshua said that there are "weightier" parts of the Law and "lesser" parts of the Law. This is an essential principle. We must discern between aspects of the Law which are more important and those which are less.

Matthew 23:23—"... you forsake the weightier aspects of the Law—justice, grace and faith."

The most important part of the Law is grace and faith, as we have already noted. The next level is justice. God punishes evil and rewards righteousness. We must not be deceived on that point (I John 3:4–8).

God has set the absolute standards of justice. What are the "weightier" sins which would receive the most punishment? They are written in the Ten Commandments.

Matthew 19:17–19—"If you want to come into life, keep the commandments....You shall not kill; you shall not commit adultery; you shall not steal; you shall not answer your neighbor as a lying witness; honor your father and mother..."

Here Yeshua clearly defines the five weightiest sins (in order of gravity):

1. Murder
2. Adultery
3. Theft
4. Lying
5. Dishonoring parents.

These are the five master, moral absolutes. They are in a category above others. They have a level of punishment above others. Murder is worse than adultery. Adultery is worse than theft. Theft is worse than lying. Lying is worse than dishonoring parents.

Believers in Yeshua ought to affirm these moral absolutes more than any other people. How much stronger the community of faith would be if we walked in these basic moral absolutes! How much the witness of Yeshua is damaged when believers gossip, use pornography, cheat, exaggerate, or complain about those in authority!

Faith and grace are strengthened by moral absolutes. May these great moral absolutes be written on the hearts of all believers, just as the New Covenant demands (Hebrews 8:10)! We should be the greatest advocates of God's absolute moral standards. The restoration of the absolute moral standards of the Ten Commandments is one of our basic mandates of these end times (Malachi 4:4).

III. Lighter Moral Law

In Yeshua's rebuke of the Pharisees, He said that we must discern the "weightier" commandments of the Torah (Matthew 23:23). If there are heavier moral laws, there are also lighter moral laws. To disobey a heavier

Anyone who believes in God must obey God's absolute moral law.

while obeying a lighter law is a perversion of justice. Even though the heavier moral law is more important, we seek to act righteously on the lighter levels as well. There are sins that deserve the death penalty; there are sins that do not (I John 5:16).

There are not simply two categories—heavy and light; there is a whole range of moral commandments of different gravity. Some of the lighter commandments would include kindness to animals, returning to a neighbor a lost article, not charging excessive interest on loans, not having marital relations during the woman's menstrual period, giving your employees enough vacation time, eating healthy food, dressing in proper attire, respecting government officials, speaking well of others behind their back, giving money to the poor, and visiting the sick.

There are countless ways to act morally in our day-to-day lives. This upright behavior is described in the Law (and in an even more detailed way in the New Covenant). All acts of integrity and compassion are an expression of faith.

IV. Biblical Symbolism

The Bible describes many symbolic rituals. In the New Covenant, those symbols are primarily immersion in water, bread and wine of communion, and anointing with oil. In the Old Covenant priesthood, there are many more symbols with many more details.

A symbol does not have meaning in itself; a symbol points to something that does have meaning. A marriage ring has meaning as long as it symbolizes marital faithfulness. To wear an expensive ring and commit adultery is a perversion.

Much of the Levitical symbols had to do with blood sacrifices. All of these sacrifices point to Yeshua's sacrifice on the cross. In that sense, faith in the cross already fulfills all the offering of blood sacrifices. In addition, there has been no Temple for the past two thousand years, so the issue of actually sacrificing is not of practical concern at this time.

There are also many biblical Holy Days. All of these calendar events have symbolic meaning. The position of the New Covenant is that we need to study and understand the meaning of these Holy Days. There is no expectation for Gentile Christians to keep these Holy Days, yet they are welcome to do so if they desire.

Torah symbolism is meaningful if one understands the spiritual significance of the symbols. Gentile Christians are not required to practice these rituals. They are permitted to do so by the leading of the Holy Spirit.

For Messianic Jews, there is a biblical calling to preserve these symbols, yet there is not a weight of reward or punishment connected to the symbols as there was in the time before Yeshua. This is because the inherent meaning of the symbols is found in Yeshua Himself.

The biblical symbols and holy days are all meaningful and significant because they point to some aspect of the kingdom of God. One is not more righteous for keeping a certain ritual; nor is he less righteous for not observing. However, understanding the spiritual meaning of the feasts and symbols can be edifying and educational to all believers, whatever their background.

V. Cultural Tradition

Many elements in Jewish tradition are called "Torah," but they are not moral laws or even biblical symbols. When biblical Law is replaced by cultural tradition, great damage is done. Some of these Jewish traditions include separating milk and meat; wearing a head covering for the men; ceremonial washing of the hands; lighting candles, etc.

I once told a dear friend who is a religious Jew, after we did the ceremonial hand washing before dinner *(Blessed are You, YHVH..., who commanded us concerning the washing of hands)*, "Well, we just broke two of the Ten Commandments. We lied saying that this was a commandment when it isn't, and we used the Lord's name in vain by doing so."

On the other hand there is great beauty and benefit in Jewish tradition in that it builds a culture and lifestyle based on reference to the Torah. This gives heritage and social guidelines in everyday spheres of activities with family and friends.

When biblical Law is replaced by cultural tradition, great damage is done.

Yeshua was zealous for the Torah. He did not rebuke religious Jews for keeping the Law but for breaking the Law. He rebuked them for replacing God's Law with men's traditions. **"Why do you transgress the Law of God for the sake of your traditions?" (Matthew 15:3).** Yeshua repeated that rebuke often. Yeshua demanded the keeping of commandments and fought against replacing God's commandments with man-made traditions.

(This is true today for every religious group. We do not want to hear Yeshua rebuke us for having broken the holy and absolute moral standards of YHVH because of our religious traditions or theologies, whether charismatic—Matthew 7:21–23—or conservative—Matthew 23:23. The Holy Spirit flows spontaneously but does not break God's moral commandments at any time.)

We are welcome to keep all cultural traditions and enjoy participating in them. Joining in someone else's culture can be an expression of love. When you love someone, you want to draw close to them and identify with them. That includes language, food, music, clothing, holidays, and everything else as long as there is no sin involved.

To the degree that we make friendship and loving relationships with people through cultural expression, it is worthwhile. Participating in someone else's culture for the sake of love and evangelism is a high commandment of the New Covenant to **"become all things to all men" (I Corinthians 9:22)**. By the same principles of love and faith, we as Messianic Jews have a calling to keep the Law as part of our identity in the New Covenant (I Corinthians 9:19–23).

When we begin to think that we are better than others because of our cultural expressions, we have crossed a dangerous line of religious hypocrisy and ethnic pride.

Let us keep the balance of these five levels of law and grace in right proportion. This Ladder of priorities is part of our "alignment."

Questions for Reflection

1. How would you translate the word *torah* in Hebrew?
2. How would you translate the word *teleioo* in Greek?
3. What are the five weightiest moral commandments described by Yeshua in Matthew 19:17–19?
4. What is the difference between symbolic law and moral law?
5. When is it right to observe cultural traditions?

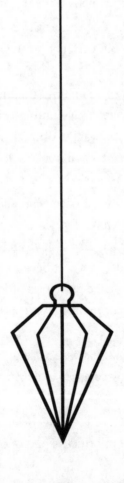

13

The Israelite Encampment

There were twelve tribes of Israel, right? No, actually there were thirteen. The tribe of Yoseph (Joseph) was split into two: Ephraim and Menashe. And the Levites were set aside to serve in the tabernacle.

The Levites carried the articles of the Holy Place and Holy of Holies on golden covered poles, right? No, actually it was only the Kohath family within the Levites.

> *Alignment has internal order which allows for outward mobilization. One of the best examples of this is the Israelite encampment in the wilderness.*

Alignment is order and direction. Alignment has internal order which allows for outward mobilization. One of the best examples of this is the Israelite encampment in the wilderness. It is the most detailed example of alignment in the whole Bible. The description is found in Numbers chapters 1 through 10. The description is very exact and somewhat complex. Every detail of the camp had a spiritual reason behind its placement and function.

Here is a simplified summary:

The camp was set up around the **tabernacle**. The tabernacle was a courtyard surrounded by a fence. The courtyard was approximately 50 meters long and 25 meters wide (about a quarter of the size of a football field). Inside this courtyard was the tent of meeting, covered by animal skins, approximately 15 meters long and 5 meters wide. The tabernacle and the entire camp faced eastward at all times.

| *It was all sensitive to the leading of the presence of the Holy Spirit cloud and the voice of the Angel YHVH who accompanied them.* |

Surrounding the tabernacle was the camp of the **Levite** families (Numbers 1:50).

Surrounding the camp of the Levites were the other **twelve tribes** of Israel.

So, there were two loops around the tabernacle, an inner smaller loop of the Levites and the wider outer loop with the twelve tribes. The tabernacle was rectangular. The surrounding encampments may have been more circular or rectangular.

In each of the twelve tribes there were approximately fifty thousand soldiers. This made the larger encampment about six hundred thousand soldiers (Numbers 1:46). Since this did not include women, children, older men, Levites or Egyptians, the total population must have been approximately two to three million people. Surprisingly the Levite tribe was only about half the median number of the other tribes (3:39).

Presumably each of the Egyptians and mixed multitude that traveled with Israel were joined to one of the twelve Israelite tribes in the encampment.

The twelve tribes were arranged facing east, going clockwise to the south, then the west and north. They were subdivided into four main camps: the first camp facing east was led by Judah (2:3); the second camp on the south was led by Reuven (2:10); the third camp in the west was led by Ephraim (2:18); the northern camp was led by Dan (2:25).

The logic of these camps had to do with the four wives of Jacob (2:2). The first four sons of Jacob were through Leah, in the following order: Reuven, Shimeon, Levy, Judah. Reuven lost his leadership by sexual sin; Shimeon lost his leadership by violent sin; Levy by cooperation with Shimeon lost the kingship but was given the priesthood.

Judah confirmed his kingly leadership of the whole family by his willingness to take Benjamin's punishment upon himself (Genesis 44:33; 49:10). Therefore, his camp led the way on the east side. Who could be the other two tribes in his camp? It could not be the three older brothers whom he displaced. It could not be one of the sons of Rachel. So it was obviously the fifth and sixth sons of Leah herself: Issachar and Zevulun. The lead camp on the east was therefore logically: Judah, Issachar, and Zevulun.

The second camp on the south returned to the family order. It was led by Reuven and then Shimeon. Who could have been the third member of their camp? There were no other sons of Leah. The sons of Rachel were not appropriate, so leadership went to Gad, the son of Zilpah, Leah's handmaid. So, the second camp on the south according to covenantal logic was: Reuven, Shimeon and Gad.

The third camp on the west side consisted of the sons of Rachel: Ephraim, Menashe, and Benjamin.

The fourth camp on the north drops down in covenant order to Bilhah (the handmaid of Rachel), Dan, and then Naphtali. Who could have been the remaining tribe? There was just the tribe of Asher, the son of Leah's handmaid. So the fourth camp on the north side was led by Dan and included Naphtali and Asher.

The encampment of the Levites around the tabernacle was also divided into four according to the four directions. Levy had three sons: Gershon, Kohath, and Merari (Numbers 3:17). The second son, Kohath, took the spiritual leadership. From among Kohath's children came Amram and then the priestly *Cohen* household of Moses and Aaron.

Therefore, the logical, covenant order of the Levitical encampment was Cohen to the east (3:38); then going clockwise was Kohath to the south (3:29); then Gershon to the west (3:23); and finally, Merari to the north (3:35).

These four families of the Levites had specific priestly duties according to the same order. Let's take the order from the outside in. The Merari family was responsible for all the outside fence of the courtyard and the boards of the tabernacle (3:36; 4:31). This was the largest quantity of material.

The Gershon family had responsibility for the tent and the **curtains** of the tabernacle (3:26; 4:24).

The Kohath family had responsibility to carry the **holy instruments** on gold-covered poles (3:31; 4:15). (They were not allowed to touch the holy articles themselves, but only carry them on poles.) They carried the ark, the showbread table, the incense altar, and the lampstand. (All these holy articles were gold covered.)

The Cohen priestly sub-family had responsibility only to carry the flour for the table, the incense for the altar, and the oil for the lampstand (4:16). There was less quantity to carry for the Gershonites than the Meraris, less for the Kohaths than the Gershonites, and less for the Cohens than the Kohaths.

How did they carry all these items? There were **six covered wagons** in the shape of turtles (Numbers 7:3). Each wagon was pulled by two bulls. Each of those twelve bulls was a donation from one of the twelve tribes. Four wagons were given to the Merari family to carry the main weight of the courtyard and boards (7:8). Two wagons were given to the Gershon family to carry the tent and curtains (7:7). The Kohaths had no wagons but only the poles to carry the holy articles. The Cohens carried only the sacraments, apparently handheld, with no need of wagons or poles.

How did the three million people in the camp know when to move? There were three levels of navigation: Moses, the cloud, and the trumpets.

There were **two silver trumpets** (Numbers 10:1) which would be blown at moments of mobilization. There were basically just two commands, or two directions: go and stop. We could call this: travel and assemble; out and in; war and ceasefire. For these two commands, there were two sounds.

The sound of *teru'ah* תתרועה was a series of short blasts. That meant to mobilize, to move out (10:5). The sound of *teki'ah* תקיעה was one long blast. That meant to gather, to camp, to assemble (10:7).

These two trumpet sounds were coordinated with the **cloud**. There was one pillar (9:15–17). It took the form of a cloud in the day so that it offered some shade and covering in the wilderness. It took the form of fire in the night so that it could offer light and heat. The divine Angel YHVH was inside the pillar.

(This glorified God-Man-Angel figure accompanied the wilderness ecclesia every day and every night for the whole 40 years. It is awe-inspiring to think that this **YHVH Angel** was actually Yeshua Himself in His pre-birth form. If so, then Yeshua accompanied the three-million-member "church" of the wilderness in person, every day, 24-7, for all those years.)

The innermost council of navigation was found in the intimate conversations between Moses himself and the Angel YHVH which took place on a regular basis. **"When Moses came into the tent of meeting to speak with Him, he heard the voice speaking to him from above the atonement cover on the ark of the testimony between the two cherubim"** (Numbers 7:89).

Moses would converse with the Angel YHVH in the tent. Then the pillar would move. The trumpets would sound. The people would take action.

The people moved according to the cloud (9:18). Sometimes the cloud would lift in the morning; they would pack up and travel all day. Every late afternoon, the cloud would have to stop somewhere for them to make camp for the night (9:21). Then the cloud would either stay in the morning or move on. Moses was most likely passing on verbal instructions to the leaders from the strategic discussions he had with the cloud Angel.

How did the mobilization work? At the sound of the trumpet, the Cohen family would immediately go into the Holy of Holies. They would take down the Holy Veil and walk forward with it to cover the ark (4:5). Then they would make sure the golden poles for the holy articles were in place and cover the rest of the holy articles with cloths and skins. Then they would take the flour, oil, and incense and leave.

The Kohaths were not allowed to touch the golden holy items (on punishment of death). After the Cohens finished, the Kohaths would lift up the holy articles by means of the poles (4:15).

As soon as they took out the holy items, the Gershon family would come in, dismantle the tent, and load all the curtains and skins on the two wagons at their disposal. Then the Merari family would move in quickly to dismantle the fence and the boards and put them on the four remaining wagons.

During this time, all the tribes were packing up quickly. The tribe of Judah would start to move out on the east, followed by Issachar and Zevulun, under the banner of Judah's camp (10:14).

Then all the six wagons and the camps of the Gershonites and Meraris would follow (10:17).

Then the southern camp of Reuven, with Shimeon and Gad, under the banner of Reuven's camp, would move out (10:18).

Then the Cohens and Kohaths with all the Holy items would follow (10:21).

Then came the camp of Ephraim from the west side, along with Menashe and Benjamin under the banner of Ephraim (10:22).

Finally, making sure that everything was gathered correctly, the northern camp of Dan, along with Asher and Naphtali under the banner of Dan, took up the rear position (10:25).

When they arrived at the next campsite, the process would reverse. The *teki'ah* trumpet would blow a long slow blast; then Judah's group would encamp; Merari and Gershon would set up the tabernacle and tent; then Reuven's group would encamp; Kohath would set the holy items in place; the Cohens would set up the veil and uncover the holy items; then Ephraim's group would encamp; then Dan's group would finalize the encampment.

Everyone had their place. Everyone knew their assigned task. Everyone was important and honored. The whole encampment could move or assemble at any time. Mobilization and activation were instant. It was all sensitive to the leading of the presence of the Holy Spirit cloud and the voice of the Angel YHVH who accompanied them. This is alignment: a covenant position for everyone; order and direction; ready for action.

(A note to end on: I am amazed at the leadership of **Moses** here. Everyone had their place. The different tribes were honored. Judah kept the leadership. There was both Levitical ministry and the priesthood. And where was Moses? He led everything from his time in the presence of the Lord. He put everyone in position except himself and his children. He was the orchestra conductor, helping the others play, without worrying about a place for himself. There was a total selflessness to Moses that allowed him to have almost unlimited authority. Ultimately his children were considered part of the Levite tribe, which was led by Aaron's family, since Aaron was Moses' older brother. Despite the huge anointing and spiritual authority on Moses, he took nothing for himself and submitted to the tribal covenantal order.)

Questions for Reflection

1. What were the functions of the four parts of the Levitical families in setting up and taking down the tabernacle?
2. What was the order of the tribes of Israel in moving out of the camp?
3. What were the two types of trumpet blasts?
4. Why was all this order described in so much detail in the Bible?

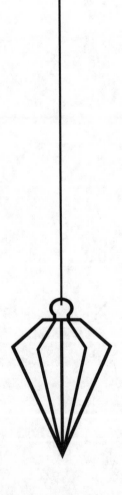

14

Sign of the Cross

We started this book in chapter one with the prayer for unity in John 17. In chapter two we talked about the prayer of God's will being done in Matthew 6. Let's put those two together as we end this section on alignment.

Did you ever notice the word "garden" in **John 18:1**? **"After He finished saying these words, Yeshua went out with His disciples across the Kidron stream and entered... into a** *garden"* **(emphasis added).**

> *The cross of Yeshua is the center*
> *of our reconciliation with God,*
> *the center of all reconciliation between man,*
> *the center of our personal faith and obedience,*
> *the center of Israel and the church,*
> *and the center of all alignment.*

Which garden was this? The Garden of Gethsemane.

What "words" had Yeshua just finished saying? The prayer of John 17.

Yeshua prayed that magnificent prayer for His disciples to become one with God and then immediately crossed the Kidron valley to pray the blood-sweating prayer of Gethsemane. The two prayers were less than one hour apart; there is a spiritual connection between them.

The prayer of Gethsemane, **"Not My will but Your will be done" (Matthew 26:39)**, was a response to the prayer of John 17. He dedicated Himself to obedience, even unto death on the cross, in order that His prayer for His disciples would be fulfilled.

Yeshua died on the cross for us to be reconciled with God. For us to

> *For us to serve God's purposes in spreading*
> *that reconciliation between God and man,*
> *and between man and man, we must also*
> *"deny ourselves, take up our cross daily*
> *and follow Yeshua" (Luke 9:23).*

serve God's purposes in spreading that reconciliation between God and man, and between man and man, we must also "deny ourselves, take up our cross daily and follow Yeshua" (Luke 9:23).

The cross is the price of unity.

Every person is called to be a bridge between two people or groups of people. How do we bring people into unity? We stand as representatives of Yeshua and demonstrate His love. People often do not want to forgive. We function as agents of Yeshua's forgiveness in prayer, dialogue, and reconciliation. This involves experiencing the pain of both sides through compassion and intercession.

"All things are from God who has reconciled us to Himself through the Messiah, and given us the ministry of reconciliation...Therefore, we are ambassadors of the Messiah; and it is as if God is pleading through us on behalf of the Messiah; be reconciled to God" (II Corinthians 5:18, 20).

If we want to be ambassadors of God's plan for reconciliation, revival and restoration, we must walk in cross-like, Christlike love. We are pierced in our hearts by love for those around us. We walk in the footsteps of Yeshua. As by the wounds of Yeshua we are healed, so do we help heal the relationships of others by standing in the gap, absorbing the hit of their anger and sin.

To align coordinates on a map or a compass, there must be a point where the horizontal axis crosses the vertical axis. The focal point on a gun sight is a cross. The center of any marked goal must be the sign of a cross.

There is something about the symbolism of the cross that marks the center of God's will. Yeshua is hanging between heaven and earth. One hand is stretching out to the east and one to the west. There is a horizontal line between man and man and a vertical line between God and man.

The sign of the cross as spiritual symbolism is quite difficult for someone who was brought up Jewish. We recently had an Israeli woman born again in our Tel Aviv congregation. She is boldly sharing her faith with all her friends. Her testimony about being baptized was so powerful that another Israeli man who had come for the first time to the congregation ended up dedicating his life to the Lord as well.

As part of her testimony, she shared that she had determined that if she saw a cross in our congregation, she would walk out immediately and never come back. The fact that we don't have crosses hanging as a symbol in most of our Messianic congregations allows for many Jewish people to understand the spiritual significance of the cross without being first offended by what seems to be a foreign, Gentile, even anti-Semitic symbol.

I sometimes tell the story of entering a Catholic church for a wedding with my dad and one of my sons. A huge crucifix was hanging from the wall with a wooden figure of Yeshua on it. The three of us stopped for a moment, and my dad leaned across me and whispered to my son, "Be careful. Look what happened to the last Jew who came into this building." (My dad, who was already a believer in Yeshua at the time, had a particularly dry sense of humor.)

I mention both of these stories to demonstrate how the symbol of the cross is culturally offensive to many Jews. In Hebrew, the word for cross and swastika (hooked cross) is the same. In Jerusalem, on some arithmetic texts for children, the cross symbol for addition is changed to a T shape. Most Jewish people have an inherent, subconscious repulsion to the sign of the cross.

Another Israeli woman asked about the symbolism of the cross as a sign. I told her there was no meaning to the sign and that she should just think about Yeshua's sacrificial love and atonement. That was the right response to her, yet something was bothering me on the inside. I sensed the Lord telling me I had missed something. That sense of inward "nagging" continued for quite a while.

One day, my wife and I went up for a hike in the mountains behind Tsora and Eshtaol (Judges 16:31). That inward nagging became very strong. I began to pray and was very perturbed. As I was praying, the forest path took us by the monument of Samson's tomb. Just as I sat down on the edge of Samson's tomb, I saw it. I saw a picture in my heart of Samson stretching out both hands as he sacrificed his life.

Then I began to think of other "hands stretched out": Moses' rod, Joshua's spear, David's prayers, Solomon's blessing, Jeremiah at the stocks, Peter's crucifixion, God "stretching out His hands all day to a rebellious people" (Isaiah 65:2) and even Zion stretching out her hands in pain (Lamentations 1:17).

Yeshua was stripped naked. His hands were stretched out in yielding and supplication. He was hanged between heaven and earth. Above His head were thorns representing His manifold authority that would later turn into crowns (Revelation 19:12). Right at the center of the cross His heart was pierced by a Roman spear. He reached toward east and west. He was centered at the focus of God's plan. The vertical and the horizontal lines crisscross over Him. The human and the divine merge together.

His feet were pierced and bleeding pointing down to the earth; His hands pierced and bleeding to the left and the right; His head bleeding upward toward the sky; His heart pierced in the middle. What incredible, incomprehensible, and all-inclusive love! What a portrait of the beauty and glory of God!

Jerusalem as a city is located at the crossroads of history and geography. Everything north of the city is "north" in world culture. The east side of Jerusalem is totally eastern and the west side is totally western. Roman, Greek, Hebraic, Aramaic, and Arabic language and culture merge at this point. Here Yeshua was crucified. Here He was declared to be "King of the Jews." His cross was located at the crossroads of human history, geography, and civilization.

Isaiah 22:22 describes the key of David's kingdom. **Isaiah 22:23** describes a stake being fastened into the ground in Jerusalem: **"I will fasten him as a stake in a faithful place and it will become the throne of glory for the house of his father."** The key, the throne, and the stake are all symbols of Yeshua's kingdom authority. This stake is also symbolic of

All resurrection life comes from Yeshua's sacrificial death on the cross.

the crucifixion of Yeshua.

That stake will become the point of alignment for the rest of the glory of the kingdom. **"They will hang upon it all the vessels of glory of his father's house" (verse 24).** The glory of our Father's house will be centered on this stake. Yeshua was tested for obedient faithfulness on the cross. His obedience was a primary reason He was given authority and glory (Philippians 2:5–11).

The stake can also be applied to our own lives personally. As each one dedicates his life to Yeshua and sacrificial loving obedience, he or she becomes a stake for "hanging the vessels" of God's grace and glory. I have tried to dedicate my life, family, and work in the image of that stake in that faithful and fateful place.

I also see the Messianic remnant in Israel as an example of that stake. This community provides a "stake-like" marker for the international ecclesia, who are the vessels of glory. This parable of the stake can be compared to the parable of the Olive Tree of Romans 11 (which we will discuss in chapter 19). The root supports and upholds the branches. Both the stake of Isaiah 22 and the Olive Tree of Romans 11 are parables of alignment, first to Yeshua, then to the remnant of Israel, and finally fully expressed in the international ecclesia.

We orient ourselves to Him and to that event. All resurrection life comes from Yeshua's sacrificial death on the cross. All revival comes because someone or some people were willing to take up their cross and follow Him. There is no spiritual glory without the suffering obedience that comes first.

Our personal point of alignment is this: **"I have been crucified with Messiah, and I no longer live, but the Messiah lives in me. The life that I now live in the flesh, I live by faith in the Son of God, who loved me and gave Himself for me" (Galatians 2:20).**

When the apostles preached the gospel, they often referred to the cross as "the tree" (Acts 5:30, 10:39, 13:29). I believe they were referring to the death punishment determined by the Torah that the guilty should be hanged on a tree (Deuteronomy 21:22) and that the cross is the remedy of the first sin of Adam and Eve at the tree of knowledge of good and evil (Genesis 3:6).

The cross transforms us from the tree of death to the tree of life. The cross will forever be our tree of life. It is on that tree we eat of the fruit of eternal life. It is by being "crucified" with Yeshua that we will bear much fruit in our own lives (John 15:2, 5).

The tree of life (as symbolized by the cross) will be in the center of Eden restored, perfect paradise for eternity. It is the intersection of heavenly Jerusalem and earthly Jerusalem (Genesis 2:9; Revelation 22:2). It is the vortex of the plan of God. It stands at the spiritual and physical center of the universe.

Let us always keep this focus. The cross of Yeshua is the center of our reconciliation with God, the center of all reconciliation between man, the center of our personal faith and obedience, the center of Israel and the church, and the center of all alignment.

Questions for Reflection

1. What is the connection between the John 17 prayer for unity and the prayer of consecration at Gethsemane?
2. How are you called personally to be in the ministry of reconciliation in your own life?
3. What is the meaning of a "stake" in a faithful place of Isaiah 22?
4. Why did the apostles refer to the cross as a "tree?"

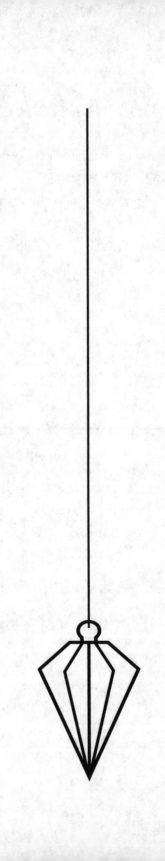

THE
ABRAHAMIC
FAMILY

*Seeing the community of faith
as the extended family of Abraham
gives us a framework
for unity and reconciliation.*

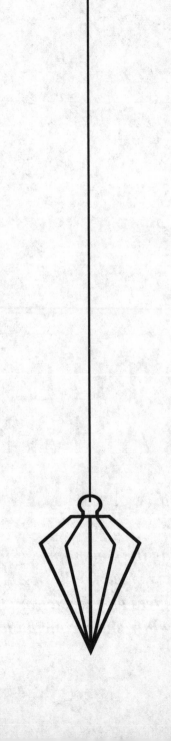

CHAPTER

15

The Heart of Father Abraham

Of all the words to describe God, the one that stands out the most is "Father" (Matthew 6:9; John 17:21). What a father wants is a family. The people of God are supposed to be the family of God.

I bend my knee before the Father who has called by name the whole family in heaven and on earth.

—Ephesians 3:14–15

The international community of faith was designed from the beginning to be an extension of the family of Abraham, Isaac, and Jacob.

God is our Father. We are His family. Notice in this verse that the family has a dual identity: in heaven and on earth. Since we are earthly beings, but created by a heavenly father, we all have that dual identity. We have citizenship in heaven as well as on earth (Philippians 3:20).

Therefore, we have to understand that our relationship as a family has a double dimension. We are spiritually children of heaven, but we also have a family identity on earth. If God had wanted only a heavenly identity, He would have created only angels, not men. Men have that double nature of spirit and body. Had God wanted only a heavenly identity, Yeshua would not have been born on the earth through a human womb.

The people of God, therefore, have this double identity, both spirituality and ethnicity. We are the international heavenly ecclesia, and we are also the extended tribal family of Abraham. The fullness of this identity could have never been understood until this generation. Today we have Asian Christians in the Far East, and Arab Christians in the Middle East, and Messianic Jews in Israel and the diaspora.

The intercultural, multiethnicity of the family of God is part of the beauty of who we are together. God has made us in many colors and many personalities.

Our heavenly identity is in Yeshua; our earthly identity as the community of believers goes back to Abraham. We are the children of the faith of Abraham. It is said of Abraham that he is: **"father to all who believe, among those who are not circumcised…and the father of those who are circumcised…who also walk in the footsteps of the faith that Abraham our father had while he was not yet circumcised" (Romans 4:11–12).**

The extended Abrahamic family includes both uncircumcised and circumcised. In other words, the earthly identity of the family of God has two dimensions within it as well: Jewish and Gentile, or more exactly: circumcised and uncircumcised.

The circumcised children of Abraham include Jews AND Arabs. We have to change our thinking in order to grasp a wider identity of the Abrahamic family. God calls us to be a family by faith which has both a heavenly and earthly identity. The earthly part of the identity starts with Abraham. Abraham's entire family includes both the circumcised and the uncircumcised. The circumcised part of the Abrahamic family includes Jews and Arabs (Genesis 17:23).

The fullness of this identity could not have been revealed until there were believers from almost every nation. The spread of the gospel in East Asia in our generation has made the "uncircumcised" part of the family openly revealed in a much larger way. The presence of Arab and Jewish believers in the Middle East is allowing the circumcised part of the Abrahamic family to be revealed for the first time in history.

There have been dramatic breakthroughs in these relationships during the "Global Gatherings," facilitated by David Demian. David himself is of

> *The intercultural, multiethnicity of the fami-*
> *ly of God is part of the beauty*
> *of who we are together.*

Egyptian origin. Through the Global Gatherings many of the Christians of mainland China, plus other nations of the world, have joined together in prayer. The Holy Spirit has brought the Arab and Jewish believers to a new level of partnership, mutual submission, and shared vision.

In the context of these Gatherings, we have experienced a release of power that is fostered by this alignment. The international church is praising God; the East Asian church is interceding; the Arabs and the Jews are reconciling. There has been an "open heaven" with a presence of the Holy Spirit for revelation and revival.

If the people of God are to have an "Abrahamic identity," obviously this could not happen until there are Jews and Arabs who are part of the family. Restoring the Arab and Jewish parts of the international family of faith is not so simple. To restore the Abrahamic roots of the family of God requires:

1. Arabs as believers in Yeshua.

2. Jews as believers in Yeshua.

3. Arabs and Jews reconciled to one another.

4. Arabs and Jews embracing international Christians as their extended family.

5. International Christians showing loving appreciation for Jewish and Arab believers due to their connection with the first family of Abraham.

(The position or role of the Messianic Jews to be affirmed in a special way by the Arab brothers and sisters is an additional dimension, which we will touch on in the next chapter.)

The five component parts of the "Abrahamic family" listed above are coming into place now in a way that was never possible before at any time in history.

The identity of the people of God is being revealed. We are the family of God. We are the faith family of Abraham. The identity of the ecclesia is being redefined in this generation right before our very eyes.

[Ecclesiology is the study of the meaning and structure of the church. We are seeing a rediscovery of the ancient covenant roots of the ecclesia. This represents a progressive understanding or redefinition of ecclesiology.]

This unveiling of the plan of God for the people of God cannot take place without the right relationship between international Christians, Arab Christians, and Messianic Jews. This alignment is happening now **"so that, by means of the ecclesia, the manifold wisdom of God will be made known to the powers and principalities in heavenly places, according to the eternal purpose He accomplished in Messiah Yeshua"** **(Ephesians 3:10–11).**

Aspects of the ecclesia are being uncovered now which have been hidden as a mystery for ages (Ephesians 2:11–3:11; Romans 11; Revelation 7). God had an "eternal purpose" for the human race, through the ecclesia, since before creation. It is a pre-determined plan.

One way to prove the "pre-destined" nature of this "Abrahamic family" definition of the international church is to note that it was promised by covenant to Abraham and his sons at the very beginning. In fact, it was promised TEN times in the Book of Genesis alone.

1. **Genesis 12:3—"In you all the families of the earth will be blessed."**
2. **Genesis 15:5—"Your descendants will be as the stars in heaven."**
3. **Genesis 17:4—"I have made you the father of many nations."**
4. **Genesis 22:18—"In your seed all of the nations of the earth will be blessed."**
5. **Genesis 26:4—To Isaac: "All the nations of the earth will be blessed in your seed."**
6. **Genesis 27:29—Isaac to Jacob: "The peoples will serve you and the nations will bow down to you."**
7. **Genesis 28:3—Isaac to Jacob: "You will become an assembly of**

> ### *Our heavenly identity is in Yeshua;*
> ### *our earthly identity as the community of*
> ### *believers goes back to Abraham. We are the*
> ### *children of the faith of Abraham.*

nations."

8. **Genesis 28:14**—to Jacob: "In you all the families of the land will be blessed."

9. **Genesis 48:19**—to Ephraim: "Your seed will become the fullness of the Gentiles."

10. **Genesis 49:10**—to Judah: "To Shiloh will be the obedience of the nations."

Notice that in all these prophecies, the language used is "family" and "tribal." The international community of faith was designed from the beginning to be an extension of the family of Abraham, Isaac, and Jacob. The Abrahamic family identity was part of that design from the beginning.

This was to be an eternal family established by blood covenant. That has never changed.

In the promise to Jacob in Genesis 28:3, the word for assembly is *kahal* קהל, which is the root of the word for "church" or "congregation" in modern Hebrew. It could have said, "You will become the church of the nations" or "you will become the international ecclesia."

In the promise to Ephraim in Genesis 48:19, we find the very phrase "fullness of the Gentiles" as was quoted by Paul in Romans 11:25. When Paul referred to the fullness of the destiny of the international Gentile church, he was quoting this prophecy to Ephraim.

(This is NOT saying that all Christians are physical descendants of Ephraim, as some wrongly claim. There were ten covenant promises that many people from all the nations would become part of the extended family of Abraham through faith. This is one prophecy in that series in Genesis. In context, the ten are all referring to the same fullness of the Gentiles.)

To embrace this vision of the nations was not easy for Abraham. In the tribal mentality of the ancient Middle East, a father was interested in his own physical bloodline. At this point, Abraham was already elderly and didn't have any children. Naturally speaking he wasn't interested in a bunch of Gentiles having an international church, to put it a bit crassly. He wanted a son to whom he could pass on his heritage and inheritance.

God chose Abraham as a man who had a great heart to be a father. He allowed him to wait decades without having a physical son. Then God showed Abraham His Father's heart for all the nations. It is as if God said to Abraham, "If you want your own family, you first have to receive in faith My heart as a spiritual father to all the nations." Abraham would only get his physical family if he would agree to adopt the Father's international family (Romans 4:18).

This change of perspective demanded a change of identity for both Abraham and Sarah. It was so great a change of identity that God had to change their names. God added the letter "H" *heh* ה to both of their names. Abram became Abraham; Sarai became Sarah.

The letter *heh* is seen symbolically to represent the name YHVH in Hebrew, as if God added His own name to their name, His identity to their identity. In context the letter *heh* refers to the word המון **hamon**, meaning multitude. On the faith side, Abraham had to have confidence that after so many years, God would still bless him and fulfill all the promises to him.

This moment of name change from Abram to Abraham was a turning point in history (Genesis 17:5). It established the covenant of a vision for an international spiritual family coming out of the family of Abraham and Sarah. It happened at the covenant of circumcision. Part of the circumcision was a commitment to be a father to the Gentiles.

I am not sure how much the fatherhood to international believers was part of Abraham's consciousness at the time. However, we do see his love for Ishmael at the time of circumcision. In any case, through the spiritual interpretation given through Paul in Romans 4, we find that being the "father of all who believe" was the central purpose of the name change from God's point of view.

In the name שרה *sarah*, the meaning in Hebrew is princess. In modern

> ### *It is as if God said to Abraham, "If you want your own family, you first have to receive in faith My heart as a spiritual father to all the nations."*

Hebrew, the word is used to mean a female cabinet member. So, in the name change there was also the receiving the promised identity of royalty. God's intentions are so overwhelmingly good for all of us. Abraham and Sarah are faith examples of the amazing grace and goodness of God.

There is a similarly difficult yet blessed and historic change of identity that God is requesting of us today. We all have to add this *heh* 'ה perspective. The church has to embrace Israel as part of her identity. Israel has to embrace the church as part of her identity. Arab Christians and Messianic Jews need to embrace one another as part of the Abrahamic family.

(I feel a similar struggle in my own heart to become a type of father, or "spiritual dad," toward the international ecclesia community. Perhaps this is a little taste of how Abraham felt. To have a family, there must be spiritual dads. This is a call to mature spiritual leaders in our generation. Will some of us become dads to this international family?)

The people of God are described in three main parables throughout Scripture:

1. A Bride
2. A kingdom
3. A family.

– The Bride is filled with the Holy Spirit for passionate love for Yeshua the Messiah as her Groom.
– The kingdom is the government of Yeshua upon the earth, reigning from Jerusalem.
– The family is the heart of love from the Father for His children to become one.

All three of these parables are essential and important. However, to my understanding, the picture of us as the family of God, united in His love as a Father, is the greatest of the three. All a father wants is for his children to love him and love one another.

[**Note:** One of the most profound revelations about God is the pain He feels as a father whose children have rejected him. When God came to His beloved children, Adam and Eve, He discovered that they had listened to lies about Him. They closed their hearts to God and rejected Him. They accused Him. They let the devil convince them that God was not worth trusting or obeying. They basically refused to talk to Him (Genesis 3:8–13).

At one point, He had to wipe out the entire human race, at the time of Noah, because all of His myriads of children had betrayed Him and become murderers and perverts (Genesis 6:5–7). The pain of God's heart is almost inconceivable. Part of the story of Job is to give an example of how God the Father felt at the partial destruction of His family by the evil influence of Satan.

The first prophecy of the Israelite prophets was actually a question posed by God. "I am your Father who loves you. Why have you betrayed Me?" (paraphrased Isaiah 1:2). The same is true of the last prophet, who asks, "I am your Father, why won't you respect Me?" (paraphrased Malachi 1:6). And the imagery extends into the New Covenant, portraying God as a father running out to hug his pig-filthy son who had betrayed him (Luke 15:20).

God allowed dear father Abraham to feel some of His longing as a dad. As we join together as a family through Yeshua the Son, as the Abrahamic family of faith, with reconciliation between all people, particularly Jews and Arabs, we are touching a place so deep in the heart of God. His family is being restored.]

Will we submit to this readjustment? Will we become God's family together? Will we receive the common roots of Abraham as our earthly father in the faith? Can we stretch our faith to see all the nations as one family? Can the Jews see the Arabs as part of their circumcised family?

> *This moment of name change from Abram*
> *to Abraham was a turning point in history*
> *(Genesis 17:5).*

Can the Arabs see the unique role of the Jewish believers in this international covenantal family? This is what circumcision means: to see by faith other people as part of your spiritual family or tribe.

If we do, I believe we will make glad the heart of our Father in heaven. Nothing would make Him happier than to see His family coming together in love and unity.

Questions for Reflection

1. How do we as followers of Yeshua have both a spiritual identity and an ethnic identity?

2. What emotional changes do we have to go through to see ourselves as the family of Abraham by faith?

3. How was the international ecclesia promised to Abraham and his sons in the Book of Genesis?

4. How has God's heart been pained by the rejection from His own children in every nation?

CHAPTER

16

Sarah and Hagar

In the 1990s after the First Intifada (1987 to 1991), discussions between Arab Christians and Messianic Jews in Israel increased. Many of the Messianic Jews tried to be sensitive to the complex situation of the Arab Christian community. Among Arab Christians there are a wide variety of viewpoints on social and political issues, particularly concerning prophecies about the reestablishment of the State of Israel.

The personal relationships between Arab Christians and Messianic Jews in Israel have always been positive (although not necessarily deep, since there are separate congregations, languages, and cultures). Some of the difficulties are not between the Jews and the Arabs themselves, but between the Arab Christians and the Christian Zionists who visit Israel and between the Arab Christians and their surrounding Arab Muslim neighbors.

> *The split and pain between Sarah and Hagar, Isaac and Ishmael, was the first division and wound in the family of God.*

In 1993, I worked with a young Arab believer by the name of Jack Sara. We became good friends. Since that time, he has grown to be one of the foremost leaders of the Palestinian Christian church and the head of the Bethlehem Bible College. Over the years, Jack and I have stayed friends despite the fact that we have extremely opposing viewpoints on the Israeli Palestinian conflict. The fact that we are good friends yet differ on these issues shows just how paradoxical the whole situation can be.

In 1995, I was requested to lead the Israeli and Palestinian delegation to

The power of Arab-Jewish reconciliation
through the love of Yeshua has the potential
to heal all other racial, political,
and religious divisions.

the Global Council on World Evangelism (GCOWE) in Seoul, Korea. We had a group of around eighteen people, mixed between Arabs and Jews. Some of the Arabs wanted to call themselves "Palestinians." We Jewish believers refused to do so. There was mounting tension within our delegation.

At the same time, there was tension with the leadership of this large convention. They did not understand the vision of Messianic Jews, nor Arab Christians. They cut us out of the weeklong program. The whole situation seemed explosive. The Arabs told me, "We Palestinian Christians agreed to call you Messianic Jews although we don't like the term. You have to call us what we choose to be called." We were still reluctant.

We went to the leadership of the conference and asked them to give us an opportunity to address the five thousand attendees. They told us there was no opportunity. We prayed hard. It was the only time in my life I felt the presence of the Holy Spirit on me physically like a blanket. I went again to the leadership and said, "I have two promises for you: we won't take too much time, and you will be pleased with what happens." They said, "Okay, you have three to four minutes."

We brought the group up on the stage. I said, "We want to introduce you to our delegation of Israeli Messianic Jews and Palestinian Christian Arabs, who…" I could barely finish the sentence. The Holy Spirit hit the room like an explosion. People fell on the floor and out into the aisles, screaming, weeping, and interceding in prayer.

I looked over at the leadership committee and raised my hands, whispering, "This isn't my fault." I stepped back off the stage and the spontaneous move of the spirit went on for over an hour. Afterwards, the leadership team came up to us and said, "We repent. That was the hand of God."

I mention all this to give one example of how dynamic the issue is of

Arab Christians and Messianic Jews serving together. We could give many other testimonies.

Muslim Evangelism

In the year 2000 came the Second Intifada. The reconciliation conferences seemed to be stalling out. We felt the Lord saying, "You need to go beyond reconciliation." We asked in prayer, "What?" We perceived the answer to be, "After reconciliation comes cooperation." So, we prayed, "In what?" The answer was: "in evangelism to Muslims."

We had an answer, but no ability—certainly no ability to do direct evangelism to Muslims. We didn't even have the faith and sacrificial love that would be required to risk our lives physically in that kind of evangelism. We began to search out Arab leaders who were interested in Muslim evangelism. We offered them our support and friendship. We said half-jokingly, "Here is our cooperation: We pray for you. We give you money. You evangelize Muslims."

Out of this came our continuing friendship with Jack, Salim, Bassem, Andreus, Brigitte, Harun, David, Nader, Samekh, Imad, Gabriel, Refaat, and many others. The testimony that Messianic Jews are standing with Arab Christians in support for Muslim evangelism has borne sweet fruit over the years.

After the outbreak of the "Arab Spring" and the sweep of violent Islamic extremism after 2011, our partnership has continued to strengthen. At one point, we said to our Arab brothers, "Oh, we are so sad about the current terrorism and extremism." They answered, "Where is your faith? We knew this had to happen. Now our people will see the real Islam without its masks. Then they will turn to the Lord." We said, "Increase our faith, Lord."

Despite the horrendous bloodshed in the decade of ISIS and Jihadic war (over half a million people brutally murdered and ten million people losing their homes), their prediction of a wave of evangelism has proved true. Multitudes of Muslims are turning to faith in Yeshua all over the world. At the time of this writing, one trustworthy estimate speaks of three million Muslims coming to faith in Egypt alone.

We have heard Arab Christians say, "The best evangelists for Christianity have been ISIS and the Jihadists. They are turning people away from Islam in large numbers."

At a recent conference with Arab Christians and Messianic Jews, I spoke on the verse from **Acts 1:7**, where Yeshua said, **"It is not for you to know the times and the seasons."** I said, "It is still not the time for Jewish revival in Israel although it is coming soon. However, we can know what the time and the season is now. It is time for the wave of evangelism to the Muslim world. I am not prophesying this but merely making an observation. In this decade, more Muslims have turned to Yeshua than in the previous thousand years. This is the time."

In the face of the enormous disasters of Islamic extremism, we are seeing continued cooperation between Messianic Jews and Arab Christians, and a wide increase of evangelism to the Muslim world.

In addition, the testimonies of joint prayer times with Messianic Jews and Arab Christians have touched many hearts in both the international and Arab Christian communities.

Ishmael First

At one Global Gathering, I was struck in the prayer time by the fact that Ishmael was thirteen when he was circumcised (Genesis 17:25). The Messianic lineage went through Isaac to Jacob to Judah, not through Ishmael and Esau. On the other hand, the family covenant of Abraham included Ishmael and the Arabs, within which are the descendants of Ishmael. There is a double order here. The Jewish people hold the covenant rights of the coming of Messiah, yet the Arabs have an integral and crucial role to play in uniting the wider Abrahamic family.

Revival among the Arab nations logically precedes revival among the Jews in Israel. As the gospel returns toward the Middle East from East Asia, it will come through the non-Arab Muslims outside the Middle East, then the Arabs in the Middle East, then the Jews in Israel. We are part way through that process now.

We have said to our Arab Christian brothers and sisters: We are con-

> *Messianic Jews and Arab Christians are forming an Isaac-Ishmael type covenant for the sake of the kingdom of God, for the sake of revival in Arab nations, and for the sake of uniting the family of God internationally.*

nected to you by faith in Yeshua and by family through our father Abraham. Our destinies are linked together. We are mutually dependent on you. God's fullness must touch your people before it touches ours.

One of the Arab pastors said, "I have been praying about the destiny of our people that goes back to Ishmael. He could have been Isaac's protective older brother. We want to fulfill that now. We recognize the prophecies about the Messianic Jews in the end times. We also recognize the spiritual attack you are under. We will stand by you. We will protect you. We will support you to fulfill your destiny." I am still trying to fathom the depth of what he said.

When we Messianic Jews speak of God's calling on us in the end times to welcome back Yeshua (Matthew 23:39), to be the "elder brothers" in the body of Messiah (Romans 11:11–24), to lead a world revival (Acts 2:17), and to restore the kingdom of Israel (Acts 1:6), it all sounds arrogant and racist. In that way, we disqualify ourselves. However, when Arab Christians stand with us and affirm God's special destiny for the Jewish people, no one can deny it.

What wisdom from God! God is using Arab and Jewish brothers to humble ourselves one before the other, and then to affirm one another. What a divine boomerang! When there is agreement between us (Matthew 18:19), then all things become possible (Mark 10:27).

The world's greatest unsolvable political problem is the conflict between Palestinians and Israelis. As Arab Christians and Messianic Jews stand together in love and unity, the power of Yeshua to solve all problems is demonstrated. This covenant partnership brings healing and unity to the family of God inwardly and revival to the nations outwardly.

The Chinese Christians refer to their vision to bring the gospel from the Far East to the Middle East as the "Road to Jerusalem." The vision for unity among Arabs and Jews in the Middle East is referred to as the "Isaiah 19 highway." Today the Silk Road from China is joining into the Isaiah 19 highway as we begin our ascent on the pathway to Zion.

Out of Egypt

Isaiah 19:23–25 speaks of a highway back and forth from Assyria to Egypt through Israel and of peace and partnership between these three nations. "Isaiah 19" has become a banner for the vision of reconciliation, partnership and blessing among Arab Christians and Messianic Jews. It is important to see Isaiah 19 in the context of the entire vision from Isaiah 2 to Isaiah 62, which stretches from Israel to the ends of the earth in the kingdom of Yeshua.

Egypt and Assyria represent the world empires with whom Israel struggled. The implications of Isaiah 19 include more than Ishmael and Isaac and their descendants.

Hagar was Egyptian. Egypt is the most populated Arab country in the world. Egypt has a major role in all the history of the Bible. At the Global Gathering in Munich in 2015, I began to see something about Egypt. Abraham went down to Egypt. Then Jacob's family went down to Egypt. Then Moses brought the children of Israel out of Egypt. In the Torah, many covenantal and historical events "came out of Egypt."

Hosea the prophet began to see that pattern. He prophesied, **"Out of Egypt I called my son" (Hosea 11:1)**. Hosea turned the historical pattern into messianic prophecy. When Yeshua was born, He was also taken down to Egypt and back. This was seen as fulfilling the same prophecy and pattern in Yeshua's life (Matthew 2:15).

I believe this pattern has a present-day fulfillment as well. Out of Egypt today will come the "spirit" of My Son and the "message" of My Son. We began to pray that a revival would break forth in Egypt and then the spirit of that revival would cross over into Israel. Out of Egypt will come the spirit of revival of Yeshua the Son into Israel.

Although we often think of the history between Jews and Arabs as starting with the incident of Sarah and Hagar, God had already sent Abraham to Egypt beforehand during a famine in order to find food and sustenance there (Genesis 12:10). God sent Abraham down to Egypt because He had a purpose for Abraham being in Egypt and a predestined plan for Jews and Arabs together, which pre-dated Sarah and Hagar.

Actually, the journey started before that when God brought Abraham from the area of Iraq and Mesopotamia; He brought him through Syria and down into the land of Canaan. God could have placed him in Canaan from the beginning. There was something that God had destined in Abraham's trip from Iraq through Israel, going down into Egypt, and then coming back into Israel.

In other words, the vision of a highway from Assyria to Egypt with Israel in the middle was a pattern set by God long before Isaiah saw it. Both Isaiah and Hosea prophesied about the future relationship between Jews and Arabs on the basis of the historical events that started in the time of Abraham. The full meaning of those prophecies is just now being revealed in our generation.

Today we are stepping into a path that was designed long before Sarah and Hagar. This relationship between Arabs and Jews through Yeshua is part of the **"good works which God prepared beforehand that we should walk in them" (Ephesians 2:10)**.

Sarah's Covenant

Let's return to the issue of Sarah and Hagar. Abraham had a covenant with God. He is the father of the family of faith (Romans 4:11). Abraham was alone. He married Sarah. The two of them were the "mother and father" of all believers. They were alone as a couple (Isaiah 51:2). Abraham and Sarah had a covenant with God and a covenant of marriage. The plan of salvation for the human race rested on these two people, their faith, and their *marriage*.

Then came the pregnancy of Hagar. What is to be done? God must remain faithful first to the marriage of Sarah and then to Hagar and her

> *It is only through the love of Yeshua that we*
> *can overcome all the enmity in our history.*

child. The issue is not whether Isaac is better than Ishmael. The issue is God's faithfulness to covenant. If God is not faithful to Abraham and Sarah's marriage, then all marriages are in jeopardy, and the covenant to bring the seed of the promised Savior is in jeopardy.

So God was forced to set priorities. Sarah comes first. Had Abraham married Hagar first, she would have come first, and the covenant of salvation would have come through her. Ishmael was circumcised first. Look at the chronological order:

1. Abraham
2. Sarah
3. Hagar
4. Ishmael
5. Isaac.

Ishmael was blessed with twelve princes in a parallel way to Isaac (Genesis 17:20). The family covenantal blessings to Isaac and Ishmael in that sense were equal and parallel. The blessing on the descendants of Ishmael has remained even today.

However, God was faithful to Sarah's marriage covenant and through her to the Messianic covenant as well. Therefore, Isaac and his offspring needed to be separated from Ishmael and his offspring.

(Over the centuries there has been a great mixture of ethnic backgrounds to what we call the "Arab" people today; certainly, it is oversimplistic to say that all are descendants of Ishmael. The Egyptian people are a mixture of Arab, North African, and a variety of other ethnic groups. All are united by the Arabic language. In some ways the blessings of the Abrahamic family have spread to them as well. Despite the difficulty in defining who exactly is "Arab" ethnically, the general pattern of God's covenant blessing can still be seen.)

Hagar and Ishmael suffered because of the struggles Abraham and

Sarah had with their own faith. Hagar and Ishmael suffered because of the divine calling on Isaac's life. The same seemingly "unfair" situation continued on between Jacob and Esau.

God is true to His word and faithful to His covenants. He was then; He is today. God was careful to preserve the marriage rights of Sarah, the protection of Hagar, the birth of Isaac, the blessing of both Isaac and Ishmael, and the coming of the Messianic seed. He will be faithful to us today as we honor His covenant order and alignment.

The split and pain between Sarah and Hagar, Isaac and Ishmael, was the first division and wound in the family of God. The wound of rejection goes so deep. It is the deepest wound in the family of God.

As this is the deepest wound, it also has the possibility for deepest healing. The power of Arab-Jewish reconciliation through the love of Yeshua has the potential to heal all other racial, political, and religious divisions.

Today, we Messianic Jews and Arab Christians are entering into a covenantal relationship through faith in Yeshua. Abraham brought Ishmael into the covenant, and he brought Isaac into the covenant. I don't know if Isaac and Ishmael themselves ever made covenant together, although they had a certain reconciliation at their father's tomb (Genesis 25:9).

It seems that we have to complete that process. Messianic Jews and Arab Christians are forming an Isaac-Ishmael type covenant for the sake of the kingdom of God, for the sake of revival in Arab nations, and for the sake of uniting the family of God internationally.

A covenant means that we are in this together. This is beyond reconciliation and beyond cooperation. Reconciliation says I forgive you for our past history. Cooperation goes beyond reconciliation and says we're willing to work together. Covenantal relationship is a third stage. We are one family together. We'll die for you, and you'll die for us. We are joining our destinies together. We're not going anywhere without one another.

As Messianic Jews and Arab Christians build these kinds of covenantal relationships, there is a significant paradigm shift taking place in the history of faith and religion, and in the covenantal foundations of Israel and the church. It also offers a solution to some of the most difficult social-political problems in the world today.

Our young Arab friends Malek and his wife, Suzan, were traveling with Betty and me in Brazil. One time he was teaching and shared about the "three love" commandments. The first is **"to love God with all your heart" (Deuteronomy 6:5)**. The second is **"to love your neighbor as yourself" (Leviticus 19:18)**. The third love is only in Yeshua: **"to love your enemies" (Matthew 5:44)**.

Malek said, "Yeshua was the only one to teach how to love someone who has been your enemy." Arabs and the Jews have been enemies for almost four thousand years even though they are cousins. It is only through the love of Yeshua that we can overcome all the enmity in our history.

Questions for Reflection

1. What is the Isaiah 19 highway vision?

2. How can the reconciliation between Arab Christians and Messianic Jews bring healing to other divisions around the world?

3. Is there a modern fulfillment to the "out of Egypt I have called My Son" prophecy?

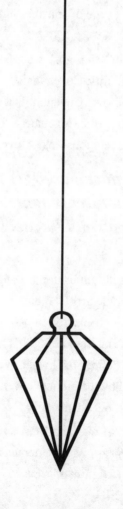

17

Rachel and Leah

Everything starts with the love of God. He creates people to love Him and love one another. A group of people that love their father (and mother) and love one another is a family. Since the family has many people in it, the family must have order so that every person will have his or her place. The community of faith is a type of spiritual family. That community has a family-type order.

Love demands covenant. The most precious part of love is intimacy. Intimacy makes for vulnerability. Covenant is to protect people from being hurt by the vulnerability of love. Covenant is a commitment to long-term relationship, loyalty, and integrity. Covenant also demands order. The covenant order is to protect the relationships of love.

> *Here is God's dilemma: Does the Messianic seed come from the covenant order with Leah or from Jacob and Rachel's romance?*

We have a standard bit of humor in our congregations. I call out in the meeting to all the young, single girls, "What does it mean when a boy says, 'I love you'?" The girls shout back, "Nothing!" I tell them that when a boy offers you a ring, then it means something. It's not just the feelings, it's the faithfulness. The covenant defines the love. Love between man and woman is supposed to be protected by the biblical covenant of marriage. The covenant is to protect all parties, but particularly the women and children.

As the old song goes, "Love and marriage go together like a horse and carriage." Love creates family; love demands covenant; both covenant and family have order. Our alignment is based on love, which is expressed

> *We are all fallible creatures upon whom*
> *God has chosen to demonstrate His mercy,*
> *patience, and grace.*

through family and covenantal order.

In the previous chapter, we talked about the covenant challenges in the family of Abraham, Sarah, and Hagar. The Messianic seed promise went on through Isaac to Jacob. Ishmael was painfully rejected, and Esau deceived. Therefore, they deserve a special place of honor in the family of God and receive special blessing. However, the Messianic seed covenant was passed on to Jacob and his sons.

At that point, the divine promise and the demonic attack are focused on Jacob's family. More detail is given to the emotional and psychological problems in their relationships than in any other biography in the Bible. They serve as a model for all the blessings of God, all the mistakes of men, and all the attacks of the devil.

Despite the problems, God demonstrates his faithfulness to this family. One way to see that faithfulness is by looking to the very end of the Bible. In heavenly Jerusalem, the gates of the city are named after the sons of Jacob. The sons of Jacob? We read in the Bible of their sins of murder, rape, jealousy, betrayal, prostitution, lying, and deceiving. How can the gates of heaven be named after them?

Somehow, as if by their very fingernails, that family barely held onto their faith. It was part heroic and part carnal; yet totally human. When we look at the story from beginning to end, we realize that the central meaning is not about their great faith or righteousness, but about the unrelenting, unwavering faithfulness of God. We are all fallible creatures upon whom God has chosen to demonstrate His mercy, patience, and grace.

The Two Sisters

At the center of the drama of this "reality show" is the relationship between Rachel and Leah. As you recall, Jacob falls head over heels in love with Rachel. He works twenty years for her as it were nothing (seven for

Leah, seven for Rachel, six for the sheep). The story is so romantic... However, at the first wedding night comes a shocking surprise. Laban deceives Jacob, who ends up with Leah instead of Rachel whom he thought he was marrying.

(How could that have happened? The rabbis try to explain that Rachel agreed to tell Leah the secret sign language that she and Jacob had arranged, so that Jacob would believe it really was Rachel. Even today carnal jokes are found in Israeli secular entertainment about lust and jealousy between the sisters.)

Here is God's dilemma: Does the Messianic seed come from the covenant order with Leah or from Jacob and Rachel's romance? It is a tough choice. God decides on the covenant order. Jacob and Rachel are still in love, and their love will have great blessing.

However, faithfulness to the covenant is not based on emotion but on order. Despite the deception and the lack of love, the fact that Jacob made a covenant first with Leah took priority. (If not, every marriage in history again would have been in jeopardy the moment one of the couple says, "Hey baby, I've lost that lovin' feeling.")

The Messianic seed did, indeed, continue on through Leah. However, the sons of Leah remained angry and jealous since they knew their dad preferred Rachel over their mother. Rachel, unfortunately, also became resentful since Leah was able to bear children and she was not. The children were born in the midst of this family feud, with all the accompanying psychological fighting and damage.

This produced a disgraceful chain of sinning one against the other. It included Leah's resentful, firstborn son sleeping with Rachel's handmaiden, and Leah's angry, second-born son murdering an entire village for having defiled his sister. Both of those sins had elements of revenge over the disgrace the sons felt over their mother not being loved by their father.

The family strife continued for centuries. Eventually it even resulted in the division of the northern and southern kingdoms: Judea and Israel. Even today there is a political conflict in Israel, bordering on civil war, between religious right-wing "Jews" and secular left-wing "Israelis"—sort of a continuance of this three-thousand-year-old contention.

The critical line of conflict comes in the relationship between Joseph and Judah. Joseph is the son of Rachel, and he, like his mom, is very loved by his dad. The fact that the favoritism passed on to the next generation totally infuriated the other (Leah-born) brothers. They wanted to kill Joseph. Eventually they feigned his death and sold Joseph into slavery.

In Egypt, because of the blessing of Jacob and because of his own integrity, Joseph prospered in all things and eventually became the leader of the entire Middle East under Pharaoh. (Notice again the positive role of Egypt protecting the Jewish brother.) Many of the Egyptians heard about YHVH, the God of Abraham, Isaac, Jacob because of Joseph. The spiritual blessing went from Jacob through Rachel to Joseph and then to the nations.

God is so faithful to Rachel that the blessing continued through Joseph to Joseph's son, Ephraim, down to Ephraim's great-grandson, Joshua, who conquered the land of Canaan. Although Rachel died tragically upon entering the Promised Land, her offspring, Joshua, years later conquered the land and even took the name of the future Messiah. (Joshua, Jesus, Yehoshua and Yeshua are all the same name.) Although her life saw many tragedies, the manifold blessings came generations later.

Rachel died in childbirth on the road to Ephrata, right outside of Beth-lehem. [It seems from the account in Luke that Miriam (Mary) gave birth to Yeshua in the same place where Rachel died. (It is interesting that Yeshua was not born in the inn, which could be a parallel to Rachel's giving birth without normal shelter.) God remembered Rachel's death and in a sovereign way prepared a way to honor her for eternity.] Orthodox Jewish girls still go to pray at Rachel's grave site on the road leading up to Bethlehem from Talpiyot, Jerusalem.

(There is also somewhat of a parable or parallel that can be seen in the lives of Leah and Rachel as compared to the history of Israel and the church.)

Judah and Joseph

The peak moment of the tension between the sons of Leah and the

> *Today we are seeing historic reconciliation between Jews and Arabs, and prophetic unity between Israel and the church.*

sons of Rachel occurred when Judah stood before Joseph (Genesis 44–45). Joseph was by then the ruler of Egypt but still unknown to his brothers. Joseph threatened to put Benjamin in jail. Judah broke down on the inside and offered to go to jail in Benjamin's place.

Judah's offer reversed the curse of the brothers' sin against Joseph right in front of Joseph's eyes. Judah became an example of the Messiah's atoning love by taking the penalty of his brothers' sin upon himself. At that moment, Joseph also broke down, burst into tears, and revealed himself to his brothers.

Both Judah and Joseph are images of the Messiah. Judah (as David's great-grandfather) represents Yeshua as the king of Israel (John 12:13). Joseph as the ruler of the Gentile world represents Yeshua as the head of the church (Ephesians 1:22). Judah has the covenant kingly rights; Joseph has the blessings of the nations.

As the tension between Isaac and Ishmael can be seen even today between the Jews and the Arabs, so can the tension between Judah and Joseph be seen today symbolically between Israel and the church. Our alignment today seeks to bring wholeness and resolution to these historic tensions. When Judah and Joseph hugged one another, the division was healed (at least temporarily). The two images of Messiah became one.

The union of the Israelite and Judean kingdoms is prophesied by Ezekiel when he holds the two "sticks" or "trees" in his hands (Ezekiel 37:15–26). (Notice the names of Judah and David on one stick and the names Ephraim and Joseph on the other stick.) We can also see this as a prophetic foreshadowing, fulfilled ultimately in the spiritual unity between Israel and the church.

This unity was also prophesied by Paul in the parable of the Olive Tree (Romans 11:17–24). (We will discuss the Olive Tree union of Israel and the church in chapter 19.) We stand in the place of Ezekiel the prophet and Paul the apostle to intercede for the healing of these historic issues. We pray for the uniting of the two sticks and for the grafting in of the branches of the Olive Tree.

It is fascinating to see that God allowed our forefathers to go through decades of suffering and tribulation in their personal lives in order to deal with a few specific character issues. Developing character is much more important to God than giving us comfortable situations. It is usually in the midst of difficult situations during an extended period of time that our character is developed.

In a family, there are different roles. One brother might be a pastor: another, an engineer. One daughter might be a stay-at-home mom; another, a bank president. Some might be believers, others, not. The rewards for spirituality are not one and the same with one's position in the family. The older brother might be irresponsible, but he is still the older brother. One sibling might take more leadership in the congregation; one in family get-togethers; and one in the family business and finances.

In ancient Israel, there was the Joseph calling and the Judah calling. There were priests, elders, and prophets. The priests and kings were each connected to a specific tribe, but the prophets were not connected to any tribe. There are many different varieties in roles in family life and spiritual life. Spiritual righteousness brings spiritual rewards. Family order preserves family blessings.

David and Mephibosheth

Let's take another example. King David was from the tribe of Judah (Leah), and King Saul was from Benjamin (Rachel). The tension was still there. Jonathan and David loved one another and made covenant with one another. At first, King Saul had both the anointing to be king and the kingly office. After he sinned, he retained the kingly office for a while, but the kingly anointing passed on to David.

Jonathan was caught between his loyalty to his dad on the one hand and his love for his friend David on the other. David respected Saul as king but had to run from him to save his own life and guard the kingdom promise. At the same time, he tried to stay faithful to his friend Jonathan.

When Jonathan and Saul were killed, David sought out the children of Jonathan. He found one remaining; a crippled boy named "Mephibosheth." David gave Mephibosheth a place at his table. The place at David's table had to do with David's love for Jonathan and his loyalty to covenant. A covenantal attitude seeks to watch over your friends' children (Isaiah 59:21). Mephibosheth had a place at David's table because of family faithfulness, not because of anything Mephibosheth had done to deserve it.

David was Leah's descendant; Mephibosheth was Rachel's descendant.

Judah First

Another issue of Leah's descendants has to do with the phrase "to the Jew first." Tribal covenant order was part of Paul's worldview as he wrote **Romans 1:16: "The gospel is the power of God for salvation to everyone who believes, to the Jew first and also to the Greek."**

The name Jew and the name Judah are the same (**Yehuda יהודה**). The idea to the Jew first comes from Genesis that the tribe of Judah was to lead. Among the twelve tribes, this was called "Judah first"—Genesis 46:28; 49:10; Numbers 10:14; Judges 1:2; 20:18, etc. Judah led his brothers. Then the tribe of Judah led the wilderness encampment. Then David's kingdom came through Judah.

This is not racial superiority of the Jews, but covenant order. As the tribes went in and out, Judah went first. In the gospel kingdom, salvation is of the Jews (John 4:22). The gospel is to the Jew first, and also to the Jew at the end. (Today the term Jew is used for all the descendants of Jacob. The Jewish people have the first right to hear the gospel according to Romans 1:16 and as seen in the pattern of Paul's ministry to always go to the Jews first.)

This is covenant order, which includes good and bad, war and peace. If the gospel comes to the Jew first, so does tribulation and persecution. **Romans 2:9 says, "Tribulation and anguish to everyone who does evil, of the Jew first and also of the Greek."** So does the judgment of God with Jews and Christians (I Peter 4:17). That is part of being "chosen." As the Jewish joke goes, "Why don't You choose someone else for a while?"

Since tribulation and anguish also come to the Jew first, we understand that the covenant order is for good and bad. Since the covenant order includes punishment as well as blessing, it cannot be an issue of racial superiority. It has to do with God's faithfulness to covenant and to the history of the kingdom of God.

The role of Jewish believers in Yeshua within the international ecclesia can reflect this covenant order. Some Christian leaders refer to the Messianic believers as "elder brother" of the ecclesia family (referencing Exodus 4:22). This is not an assertion of governmental leadership over the church by racial preference, but a recognition of historic covenantal order and alignment.

Just as in the encampment of Moses, how will the greater body of Christ today know how to be mobilized, move out, and reassemble if the tribe of Judah is not in place? The trumpet must blow a clear sound in order to mobilize for warfare. **First Corinthians 14:8 says, "If the trumpet does not blow a clear sound, who will prepare for battle?"** If there is not a prophetic understanding of the role of the Jewish believers as "Judah first," there cannot be a clear mobilization for spiritual warfare in the end times. Again, we are speaking of spiritual alignment, not a governmental role in an overarching church organization.

God's Faithfulness

God's faithfulness continued on through the generations. When we come to the New Covenant, it is astonishing to note that Yeshua is the son of Judah; John the Baptist the son of Levy; and the Apostle Paul the son of Benjamin. The roles may change, and the blessings change, but God's faithfulness to His family covenant goes on forever.

[It is ironic that the Apostle Saul (Paul) and King Saul were both descendants of Rachel. David and Yeshua were both descendants of Leah. I imagine that Paul may have noticed that he persecuted the followers of Yeshua just as King Saul persecuted David and his followers. He repented deeply and became the fulfillment of Jonathan, the beloved friend of David.

I can think of no more tragic figure in the Scriptures than Rachel. How could such a beautiful love be so frustrated and disappointed. She died in childbirth. She saw none of the covenant promises come to pass. Yet her great-great grandson became the apostle to the nations. In some ways almost all Christians owe their salvation to the zealous ministry of the Apostle Paul.

I imagine that one day, Rachel will awake in the resurrection, and she will turn to see hundreds of millions of people who refer to her lovingly as "mother" or "mommy" for the rest of eternity. From the love of Jacob and Rachel came the largest part of the family of God from the multitude of the nations. I can almost see God smiling and looking at Rachel, saying, "You didn't think I would let you down, did you?"]

These same issues concerning covenant, loyalty, faithfulness, integrity, and family order are relevant as we seek to be aligned with God's purposes for us today. We are still learning our own character lessons. God is still looking to bring reconciliation between the sons of Ishmael and the sons of Isaac, and to bring Israel and the ecclesia to their fullness and unity.

We are part of the Abrahamic family of faith. Today we are seeing historic reconciliation between Jews and Arabs, and prophetic unity between Israel and the church. This is all starting to happen right before our eyes. Seeing the community of faith as the extended family of Abraham gives us a framework for unity and reconciliation.

Questions for Reflection

1. Why does love demand covenant, and covenant demand order?

2. What can we learn from the difficult biographies of the family of Abraham, Isaac, and Jacob about spiritual warfare? About the faithfulness of God?

3. How does the covenant order of "Judah first" give meaning to the phrase that the gospel is to the "Jew first?"

4. How does the tension between Judah and Joseph reflect the history of Israel and the church?

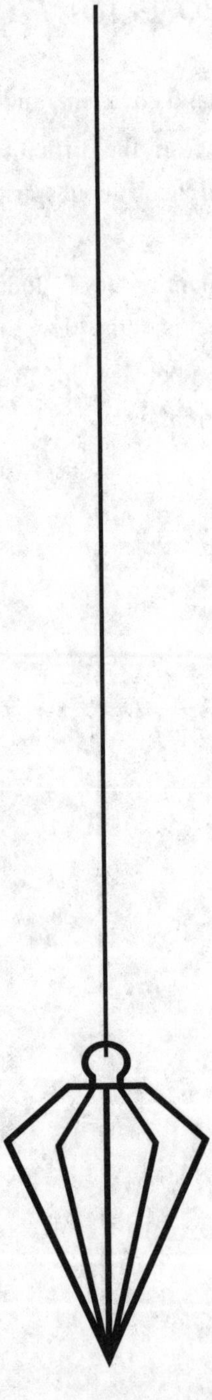

RESTORATION OF ALL THINGS

Now is the time for the completion of the
Great Commission, for the outpouring of the Spirit
on all flesh (Acts 2:17–21), and for the restoration
of all things (Acts 3:20–21).

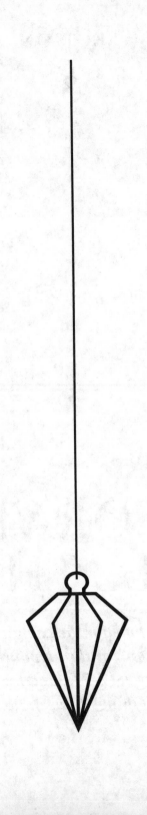

18

A New Age of Apostolic Action

The year 2017 was the five hundredth anniversary of the Protestant Reformation and the fiftieth anniversary of the unification of Jerusalem. The year 2018 was the seventieth anniversary of the founding of the State of Israel. I have sensed in my heart the Holy Spirit saying that since that time we have a special opportunity to "return to a new age of the acts of the apostles."

For decades, we have looked to the book "Acts of the Apostles" as the pattern for ministry. Now we are to go deeper: more than simply emulating a biblical pattern, we are entering into a similar or parallel time period.

We are entering a new age where the apostolic and the apocalyptic will intersect.

In 2004, when we started "Revive Israel," Acts 1 served as the model for our team to walk in a similar pattern of prayer, power of the Spirit, and world evangelism. At Ahavat Yeshua in Jerusalem, we have held Acts 2 as the pattern for congregational life. At Tiferet Yeshua in Tel Aviv, we saw a promise for a revival as in the days of Peter, as recorded in Acts 9:35, 38 (Jaffa, Lod and Sharon as mentioned in these verses is the area known as Tel Aviv today). At Tikkun Global we seek a cooperative unity with other international networks based on the model of the council meeting in Acts 15 and the "restoration of all things" in Acts 3:21.

Those are just examples of how we look to the Book of Acts as a model from which to find a strategic pattern to serve the Lord. Many other restoration-oriented ministries look to the Book of Acts as a model for their work in the same way that we do.

The overlap of these two "apocalyptic-apostolic" windows of time should help clarify some of the confusion as to the timing of end times prophecies.

However, this discernment to "return to a new age of the acts of the apostles" adds another dimension of spiritual significance. We are not just to return to the Book of Acts as a pattern, but to come into a period of time, an age, which is parallel yet greater than the age of the apostles in the Book of Acts.

[Peter spoke of the promised end times' outpouring in Acts 2:17; and Paul wrote of "greater riches" at the time of the restoration of Israel in Romans 11:12.]

In referring to that first age of the apostles, Paul wrote in **I Corinthians 10:11: "to us upon whom the end of the ages has come."** What age and what end was he talking about?

The Holy Spirit was poured out at Pentecost in AD 33. The apostle Paul was beheaded in AD 67 and the city of Jerusalem destroyed in AD 70, by which time the explosive revival of the Book of Acts had already scattered. There was a relatively short window of time between AD 33 and AD 70 in which all the "action" of Acts took place. All the events of the Book of Acts occurred in less than thirty-seven years.

The "end of the age" that Paul wrote of was the destruction of Jerusalem in AD 70. There was a previous "end of the age" at the destruction of the first Temple in 586 BC and one previous to that in Noah's time (II Peter 3:5–10). There will be another "end of the age" at the second coming, and yet another at the end of the millennial kingdom (Revelation 20).

Yeshua, Peter, Paul, and John all spoke of two different "ends"—one in their own generation at the destruction of Jerusalem and the one that would take place much later at the second coming. That second "end of the age" seems about to occur in our generation as we draw closer every day to Yeshua's return and the events leading up to it (Matthew 24:3).

When one reads the prophecies of the end times in the Gospels and the Epistles, there is an overlap of these two "ends of the age." Both of these key apostolic ages involve the destruction of Jerusalem. The first age of the apostles occurred right before the "end of the age" in their time when Jerusalem was destroyed. This new age of "Book of Acts" type ministry happens right before the "end of the age" in our time, in which all the nations of the world attack Jerusalem to destroy it (Zechariah 14).

The first apostolic age took place right after Yeshua's ascending into heaven from earth. We are in the period shortly before His descending from heaven back to earth. A unique factor in these two time periods is the **<u>overlap</u>** of the international ecclesia and the Messianic community in Israel. Before AD 33 there was no ecclesia. After AD 70, there was no Israel. During that one generation, both the ecclesia and the remnant were in position. For the first time in two thousand years, the coexistence of these two bodies has come back into place.

The first age of the apostles lasted from AD 33 to AD 70. The end of that age and the revival took place in a relatively short time. In our generation, the conditions of the Book of Acts are lining up again. There is an alignment taking place now between the international ecclesia and the Messianic remnant in Israel. There was no opportunity for this alignment to take place in previous generations since AD 70.

The first age of the apostles was a transition time between two para-digms. It was the overlap between the two-thousand-year period of the nation of Israel and the two-thousand-year period of the international ecclesia. It was a birthing time. It was a time of tribulation and of miracles. It was a time of the change in the dispensations of the kingdom of God. For that transition to take place, Israel, the church, and the Messianic remnant had to exist at the same time.

The overlap period of the ecclesia and the Messianic remnant was the age of the apostles upon whom the end of their age had come. Now we are entering again into a unique and parallel period of time. This is the transition birthing stage before the second coming of Yeshua and the millennial kingdom on earth. There is once again an overlap of the international ecclesia and the Messianic remnant for a new period of apostolic and prophetic ministry before the end of this age.

In the transition between ages, there is an increased pace of communications and revelatory understanding. The "seals" of the plan of God begin to open quickly. In the first Apostolic age, the New Covenant was written, the Spirit poured out (Acts 2:1–4), and the Great Commission launched (Acts 1:6–8).

Now is the time for the completion of the Great Commission, for the outpouring of the Spirit on all flesh (Acts 2:17–21), and for the restoration of all things (Acts 3:20–21). This transition time will include the traumatic events of the end times as well. The apostolic and the apocalyptic are being joined together.

In other words, the great revival of the end times is necessarily connected to the tribulation of the end times, which is necessarily connected to the events leading up to the second coming. There was a relatively short transition time in which apostolic events in the Book of Acts coincided with the terrible events leading to the destruction of Jerusalem. At the very end there will be a parallel apostolic-type age coinciding with the apocalyptic events described in the Book of Revelation.

The apostolic and the apocalyptic are beginning to come together. We read the Book of Acts and the Book of Revelation. These two "tracks" will merge. The type of events in the Book of Acts will return. This will happen during the events prophesied about in the Book of Revelation. That will be the end of this age. The apostolic events of the Book of Acts will merge with the apocalyptic events of the Book of Revelation.

This overlap should be clear when we read the prophecy of Joel 2 and Acts 2: *In the end times God will pour out His spirit on all flesh. There will be signs and wonders in the heavens and on the earth. This will take place right before the great and terrible day of YHVH.*

The overlap of these two "apocalyptic-apostolic" windows of time should help clarify some of the confusion as to the timing of end times' prophecies. The problems are three-fold:

The second apocalyptic apostolic age will come in the time leading up to the second coming.

1. The New Covenant prophecies seem to be talking sometimes about the destruction of Jerusalem in the first century and sometimes about the second coming of Yeshua.

2. The teachings of the New Covenant say we are to know the times, but then say we are not to know the times.

3. The timing of the coming of the end is sometimes said to be very near, and sometimes to be very far away.

The apostolic-apocalyptic window takes place right before the destruction of Jerusalem and also right before the coming of the Messiah. The attack of the nations on Jerusalem is always THE apocalyptic event. At that event, either the Lord intervenes in victory, or He allows the nations to destroy the city.

This event happens four times: three times in the past; one time in the future. (Actually, this event happens a fifth time if we include the attack of Satan at the end of the millennium in Revelation 20.) Here are the four, one victory and one destruction in the Old Covenant; one victory and one destruction in the New Covenant:

1. Victory—Isaiah 37—12 BC—Sankheriv (Sennacherib)

2. Destruction—Jeremiah 39—86 BC—Nebuchadnezzar

3. Destruction—Luke 21—AD 70—Titus

4. Victory—Revelation 19/Zechariah 14—AD 20??—Antichrist

In the time of Isaiah-Hezekiah, the nations led by Sankheriv of Assyria attacked Jerusalem. The people prayed for help. The Angel YHVH intervened at the very last moment, killed 185,000 people in one night, and saved the city (Isaiah 37; II Kings 19; and II Chronicles 32). That is the historic biblical precedent for the coming of the Messiah in a sudden apocalyptic victory.

The second time happened in the time of Jeremiah (586 BC). The people and the king did not listen or repent. The nations led by Nebuchadnezzar of Babylon attacked Jerusalem. The punishment visitation of the Lord was at hand. This was their apocalypse. Jerusalem was destroyed and the people exiled (Jeremiah 39; 52; II Kings 24). That was the historic biblical precedent for judgment of God upon Jerusalem.

The third time happened in AD 70. Another time of visitation, punishment, destruction, and exile was at hand (Luke 13; 19; 21). The people rejected Jesus' words just as Jeremiah's words were rejected in a previous generation. The apocalyptic disaster took place with no saving intervention.

The fourth time is yet to come. This is the time of the second coming. The nations will attack, led by the Antichrist. Revival will take place first and people will turn to the Lord in repentance and prayer. Then Yeshua will intervene as the Angel YHVH and save the nation (Revelation 19; Zechariah 14).

The time of exile had to take a long time because the gospel of the kingdom had to reach all the nations (Matthew 24:14). If we had been told clearly that it would take a long time, the urgency and motivation would have gone down. So, all the "timing" exhortations of the New Covenant have the same meaning:

The situation is urgent, but it will take a long time. Behave as if the end will come tomorrow even though it will take so long. Be diligent and alert and persevering. It will seem like a long time, but in the perspective of eternity, it is just a short moment. The situation is urgent; the battle is long. The second apocalyptic apostolic age will come in the time leading up to the second coming.

The worldwide revival will culminate in a revival in Israel. The revival in Israel will come at the end of a process. That process has already begun. I would see it this way:

1. First "some" will be saved (I Corinthians 9:22).
2. Then 7,000 will be saved (Romans 11:4–5).
3. Then 144,000 will be saved (Revelation 7:4).
4. *Then "all Tel Aviv" will be saved (Acts 9:35, 42).*
5. Then all of Israel will be saved (Romans 11:26).

Tel Aviv!? Well, the Book of Acts does not say Tel Aviv because the name of the modern city only came into use at the turn of the 1900s. However, the north part of Tel Aviv is called Sharon; the east part of Tel Aviv is called Lod; and the south part of Tel Aviv is called Yafo. (The west is the Mediterranean Sea.)

It was to that specific area that Shimon Kefa (Simon Peter) arrived to do some of his most outstanding miracles. In Acts chapter 9, it is recorded that he healed a paralyzed man named Aeneas and then raised from the dead a woman named Tabitha. In response to those miracles, there was a massive revival in the whole area.

Acts 9:35—"All those who lived in Lod and Sharon saw him [Aeneas] and turned to the Lord."

Acts 9:42—"And it [the raising of Tabitha] became known throughout all Yafo and many believed in the Lord."

All Sharon, all Lod, and all Yafo turned to the Lord. That is all Tel Aviv. It happened then. It can happen again. The Book of Acts is our historical pattern, and it is our prophetic hope. Using a similar terminology to that of Peter and Paul, we could say, "All Tel Aviv will be saved, and then all Israel will be saved."

The Holy Spirit was poured out in fire on the day of Pentecost in Acts 2:1–4. In response Peter prophesied from the Book of Joel that there would be a worldwide revival in the end times in the same way that it happened to them. The Acts 2:2 "pattern" became the Acts 2:17 "prophecy."

Some Bible scholars speak about the kingdom as having come in an "already, but not yet" way. Similarly, Joel was fulfilled in an "already but not yet" way, in the first century and then in a fuller way right before the second coming.

[We mentioned previously the enlightening connection between the Joel prophecy and the Book of Acts. In **Acts 1:6** the disciples asked, **"Will you at this time restore the kingdom to Israel?"** In some sense, they were quoting **Joel 3:1: "At that time I will restore the captivity of Judah."** That is part of the prophecy of the outpouring of the Holy Spirit on all flesh in the end times (Joel 2:28; Acts 2:17).

The disciples asked when Israel would be restored. The Holy Spirit is promised to be poured out on all flesh in the end times at the same time that the kingdom is restored to Israel. So, the answer to the first question of the disciples is that the kingdom will be restored to Israel as part of the end times' revival right before the second coming. This is the age we live in.]

We are entering a new age where the apostolic and the apocalyptic will intersect. Pattern becomes prophecy. The scriptural pattern of the Book of Acts becomes living prophecy for us today. This is a renewed type of apostolic age.

Questions for Reflection

1. What are some of the special elements of the period of time from AD 33 to AD 70?

2. What of those "overlapping" elements are recurring today?

3. What does a united attack by Gentile nations against Jerusalem have to do with the biblical concept of "the end of the age?"

4. What does it mean that "the apostolic and the apocalyptic are coming together?"

19

Romans 11 Revisited

If there is any one chapter in the Bible that speaks most clearly of the right alignment between the Messianic Jewish remnant and the international church ecclesia, it is Romans 11. I first taught on Romans chapter 11 when I was sent out by Jewish evangelist Manny Brotman in 1978. I was a believer of only one year at the time. Manny told me to teach on the "Romans 11 Message." After four decades, I am still amazed by the depth of revelation in this chapter.

Let's revisit Romans 11 in these five dimensions:

1. Main Subject
2. Historical Process
3. Reorientation
4. Final Result
5. Spiritual Principle.

> *If there is any one chapter in the Bible that speaks most clearly of the right alignment between the Messianic Jewish remnant and the international church ecclesia, it is Romans 11."*

The main subject has to do with the relationship between the Messianic remnant of Israel and the international church ecclesia. The relationship between them is described by the parable of the Olive Tree. The picture of the Olive Tree is perhaps the best example in all Scripture of the global alignment that we have been speaking about.

[There are three "arbor" (tree) parables in the New Covenant: **The Fig**

Tree is *national Israel* (Matthew 24); the **Grape Vine** in the Hebrew Bible is Israel but is applied as the *ecclesia* (John 15); the **Olive Tree** (Romans 11) focuses on the *Messianic remnant*. In the Romans 11 olive tree, ancient Israel is the root. The natural branches are the Messianic remnant, and the grafted-in branches are the believers from all the nations.]

The historical process of the growth and cultivation of the Olive Tree covers two to three thousand years. It starts with a Jewish root and branches. Then the Jewish branches are broken off with Gentile branches grafted in. Then the Jewish branches are grafted back in.

After the Israelite branches are re-grafted into the tree, the tree returns to its original root. The two types of branches are united, and the Olive Tree becomes identified as the tree "belonging" to the "natural" branches. There is a reorientation towards its original identity.

When the Olive Tree comes into right alignment, the final result is massive revival and restoration. The reorientation causes life from the dead (Romans 11:15), the fullness of the Gentiles (verse 25), and revival in Israel (verse 26).

The guiding spiritual principle in the process is mutual submission and humility. The humility here is a reversal of ethnic pride. Ethnic humility of both Jew and Gentile, of both Israel and the Nations, brings everyone into global alignment and a manifestation of the glory of God.

This racial humility is in direct opposition to "chosen-ness" in the sense of racial superiority. Jewish and Christian destiny is redefined by serving one another. One of the central prayers in Judaism is "Blessed are you, O God, who has chosen us from all the peoples." We change the "from" to "for."

Let's summarize the five parts:

1. Subject: Relationship of the Israel remnant and the international ecclesia

2. Process: Israel to the remnant to the ecclesia to the remnant to Israel

3. Reorientation: Olive Tree returns to original identity

4. Result: Revival and restoration in the end times

5. Principle: Unity, Humility and Mutual submission.

Let's walk through the passage now that we already know the conclusion. The chapter starts with a reasonable question. Considering the rapid growth of the international church and the impending destruction of Jerusalem, is there a continuing destiny for Israel?

The answer is an unequivocal "yes." Or in the Scriptural language: **"Has God cast away His people? Certainly not!" (Romans 11:1).** Despite the historical situation, God has a continuing glorious destiny for the people of Israel.

Israel's present incomplete state will one day turn to full restoration, for: **"God is able to graft them in again" (Romans 11:23).**

Israel as a nation does have a calling. That calling is pre-destined: **"His people whom He fore-knew" (verse 2).** The calling is based on something that will yet happen in the future because God knows ahead of time what will happen in the end.

The destiny of Israel is not found in the "unbelieving" majority but in the "grace" minority: **"the remnant according to the election of grace" (verse 5).** The destiny of the nation cannot be fully understood by looking to unbelieving politicians, generals, or rabbis alone.

Divine destiny is always in the remnant. That is true for China, for the United States, for Uganda, Poland, Guatemala, Qatar, or any other nation. The DNA of any nation's divine destiny is found within the believing remnant, not in the majority part of the society. The remnant of grace is almost always in the minority. In every nation, there is an internal struggle between the carnal culture and their divine destiny.

Those two characteristics are parallel but opposite. The church of Brazil has an amazing gift of fellowship and joy. On the reverse side, you find "Carnival." The calling of the church of China is the parallel but opposite of Communist dictatorships. The calling of the Arab church is the parallel but opposite of Islamic Jihad. Contrary to our own racial pride, the destiny of Israel is to serve and bless the Gentile nations (Genesis 12:3).

> *The picture of the Olive Tree is perhaps the best example in all Scripture of the global alignment that we have been speaking about.*

We can see a parable of this dual ethnic identity in the pregnancy of Rivka (Rebecca). She had two twin nations inside of her (Genesis 25:23). Every nation has a twin personality: divine destiny in the weaker, smaller twin; and carnal culture in the stronger majority twin.

Paul is defining here the destiny of Israel. As a rabbi within Israel, Saul (Paul) is explaining what it means for Israel to be the chosen people. The calling of Israel:

1. is pre-destined by God;
2. is found in the remnant;
3. will be restored in the end times;
4. its primary purpose is to bless the Gentiles.

Paul affirms that the chosen calling of Israel continues into the future. **"The gifts and callings of God are irrevocable" (Romans 11:29).** This principle is well described by Dan Juster in his book *The Irrevocable Calling*.

In a way similar to Jewish mysticism, Paul makes the radical claim that the punishment and exile of Israel actually has a *redemptive* purpose. Kabbalist mysticism holds that bits of light were scattered into the Gentile nations at the exile and will be regathered at the restoration of the nation of Israel.

Like all the prophets of Israel, Paul agrees that the exile was caused as punishment for our sin. Yet he also states that despite our sin, God had a secret purpose which was to *bless* the Gentiles. **"Their falling was for the salvation of the Gentiles" (Romans 11:11).** What a radical statement! The sovereign grace of God will bring redemption even out of our failure.

The second redemptive purpose of the exile is that the blessing and growth of the Gentile ecclesia would ultimately cause spiritual jealousy among the Jewish people and motivate them to return to their own faith. The Gentile church is supposed to **"make them [Israel] jealous"** **(verse 11)**.

Then Rabbi/Apostle Saul gives yet a third reason: the restoration of Israel after their falling away will be even stronger than their original calling. **Verse 12: "If their falling away was riches for the Gentiles, how much more will their restoration be!"** The restoration of the end times' Messianic remnant will be greater than the first-century apostolic community.

Paul goes on to describe several other redemptive purposes: The Jewish people will be taught the depths of humility and the grace of God (verse 6). Jews and Gentiles will learn to serve one another (verses 17–22). The Gentiles will be humbled by understanding the calling of the Jews (verse 25).

God will use the exile of Israel, the history of the church, and the restoration of Israel, to show that both Jews and Gentiles have fallen short. Ultimately, we are all being shown mercy and grace: **"God has shut them all up in disobedience in order that He might have mercy on everyone" (verse 32).**

God uses the Olive Tree partnership of Israel and the church to bring about a better world in which there is no racial superiority or ethnic pride. There will be humility, mutual respect, and dependence on the grace of God.

How can we respond to all this sovereign direction of God throughout the history of Israel and the church just to show us His mercy and grace? **Verse 33: "Oh, the depth of the riches of the wisdom of God!"**

To receive this grace of God, both Jew and Gentile need to come to a place of humility. The Jews are brought to humility by the two-thousand-year exile. The Gentile church is brought to humility by the special place of Israel in the "Olive Tree" plan of God.

Romans 11:25: "Brothers, I do not want you to be ignorant of this mystery, lest you be wise in your own eyes." The revelation about Israel's destiny guarantees the humility of the Gentiles. In some ways, verses 17 through 24 may be seen as a rebuke to the Gentile church to keep them humble. The rebuke goes in both directions: to bring both Israel and the church into their mutual humility and unity.

What specific aspect of this plan causes humility for the Gentiles? It is not that the Jews can return to be part of the church. There is no Gentile humility in that. The stumbling block for the Gentiles is to realize that there is still a divine calling for the Messianic remnant in the international ecclesia. The Jews still have an irrevocable calling, such that without them, the church cannot attain its fullness (Romans 11:29; Ephesians 3:3–10).

The Jewish part of the humility is apparent in the rejection of Messiah, destruction of Jerusalem, exile to the nations, and the need for the Gentiles to help bring them back to their own salvation.

So, there is a mutual humility for the Gentiles and Jews to recognize their need of one another. **"Do not boast against the branches. If you boast, know that you do not support the root, but the root supports you" (verse 18).** Of course, Yeshua is the ultimate "root" according to Isaiah 11:1, but this verse would make no sense if it meant, "Yeshua supports you."

The context of the whole passage is the relationship between the Messianic remnant and the international ecclesia. This verse is calling the international ecclesia to recognize that the Messianic remnant has a "calling" like a root. (Also compare Isaiah 60:21, which describes the Israel remnant as the root.)

The root is supposed to make the branches "holy" (verse 16); to give the branches spiritual life and "sap" (verse 17); and to "support" (verse 18). This is somewhat embarrassing for us as the Messianic community because we have largely failed in that purpose. However, according to the Olive Tree parable, that situation should improve in the near future.

Is more humility needed for the Messianic remnant to serve, support, and bless, or for the international ecclesia to receive from them? Or for the Messianic remnant to realize we wouldn't even be here if not for the church? All the perspectives are equally humbling. The Olive Tree is a picture of mutual blessing and mutual serving.

The last step of reorientation is the most difficult. It is found in the

Ethnic humility of both Jew and Gentile, of both Israel and the nations, brings everyone into global alignment and a manifestation of the glory of God.

phrase "their own" in **Romans 11:24: "How much more will the natural branches be grafted back into their own olive tree?"** It is not the "grafting" that is problematic but the "ownership." How can the olive tree of all the nations be "their own?" This is a major reorientation for both the Messianic remnant and the international ecclesia.

It is an issue of identity. Does the church "belong" to Israel, or does Israel belong to the church? Is the ecclesia "part" of the commonwealth of Israel (Ephesians 2:12)? Is Israel "part" of the global ecclesia of nations? Who is part of whom? The answer to all those questions is "both."

When a child is adopted or a woman married, they take on the name and identity of the family. According to the Olive Tree parable, the Messianic remnant is to see the international ecclesia as "its own" family. This is essentially a fulfillment of God's original prophecy to Abraham of blessing all the nations (Genesis 12:3).

Who is taking "ownership" or "adoption" of the international ecclesia? Who has the calling to protect, serve, unite, bless, revive, sanctify? The answer goes in both directions. How will the ecclesia become a family and fulfill her destiny? Yeshua Himself is the head of the church and the king of Israel. We are called to serve one another.

The Israelite branch is the only branch on earth which has common historic roots to all the other branches of the international ecclesia. Yeshua is the root, but He decided to build the church by starting with a group of Israeli disciples. This is part of His design.

None of us as believers in Yeshua are racist in the more obvious, grosser sense of the word. However, there is a subtle aspect of racial pride that is much more difficult to detect in oneself. This racial pride sees the positive aspects of our culture and identity. We see our good points as the

Divine destiny is always in the remnant.

"universal" good points that all other ethnic groups should conform to.

We tend to dismiss the gifting of other ethnic groups as secondary. We categorize other people in such a way as to consider them less important. In Peter's amazing vision of the sheet with unclean food in Acts 10 and 11, God told him not to call other people "unclean" or "defiled." May God free us from the tendency to see other people groups as less significant than our own!

Will the Messianic remnant escape from self-centeredness and start serving the ecclesia? Will the ecclesia receive a unifying and servant-leadership role for the Messianic remnant? The Messianic remnant is to help the international ecclesia come to her fullness. The ecclesia is to help Israel come to her fullness. There is perfect balance in God's plan.

This is the double humility that is needed for us to come into right alignment. This is the picture of the Olive Tree. And what will be the result of this partnership? Romans 11 promises: fullness for the church (verse 25); revival for Israel (verse 26); and resurrection from the dead (verse 15).

Questions for Reflection

1. How would you describe the meaning of the symbolism of the Olive Tree's root and branches?
2. How does the parable of the Olive Tree bring mutual submission and joint identity between Israel and the church?
3. How is the spiritual DNA of every nation contained within the believing remnant of that nation?
4. Does the Olive Tree parable mean that the Messianic remnant should have a role to play in uniting the international church?

20

The Restoration of All Things

Romans chapter 11 twice mentions the word fullness, **pleroma** in the Greek. Once it refers to the fullness of Israel (verse 12) and once to the fullness of the Nations (verse 25). This is the promise of **double fullness!** Both of these two will come to their fullness together, then the plan of God will be completed.

Neither the church nor Israel can bring the kingdom of God; just as neither a man nor a woman can have a child alone. The marriage of man and woman brings a child; the partnership of Israel and the church brings the kingdom of God. I summarize this in a little formula: Israel plus the church equals the kingdom of God (I + Ch = KoG).

In the beginning the Garden of Eden was a perfect paradise. In the end, that perfect paradise will be restored and even better.

Romans 11:25—"Hardness of heart has happened to Israel in part until the fullness of the Gentiles has come in."

The fullness is more than just a certain number being saved. It is God's full plan for the Gentile nations which, as we noted, was prophesied <u>ten times</u> in the Book of Genesis. The fullness of the Gentiles in Genesis was connected to the people of Israel in all ten references. Israel and the nations were destined to be together. Derek Prince used to refer to this as the "parallel" restoration of Israel and the church.

The nations come to their destiny through the fullness of the international ecclesia. The ecclesia is the full *pleroma* of the nations of the world.

> *When Israel and the church come to their*
> *fullness, they cooperate. In their partnership,*
> *they invite Yeshua to return.*

The fullness of the ecclesia then causes something else to happen.

Romans 11:26—"And so all Israel will be saved" (11:26).

The words "and so" indicate a causative reaction. The fullness of the ecclesia causes the revival in Israel. The revival in Israel is dependent on the Gentile church. When revival takes place in Israel, then Israel comes to her fullness.

Romans 11:12—"If their fall was riches for the world and their loss riches for the Gentiles, how much more will their fullness be?"

The fullness of Israel is found in the fullness of the Messianic remnant in Israel. The fullness of the remnant in the end times will be "much more" than the apostolic revival of the first century and much more than the international church at this stage of time. This is what we call the "greater riches" promise.

The words *fullness* and *restoration* are used in a parallel way in verses 12 and 15. The "fullness" and the "restoration" are part of the same concept.

Romans 11:15—"If their rejection was reconciliation for the world, what will their restoration be but life from the dead."

The reconciliation of the world takes place through the international ecclesia. Yet something more is coming. When Israel and the church come to their fullness, they cooperate. In their partnership, they invite Yeshua to return. Since Yeshua is both king of Israel and head of the church, they *both* need to invite Him to return. When He returns, He drives the devil and demons off the planet and brings about the first resurrection (Revelation 20).

At that point Yeshua sets up His kingdom from Jerusalem to the ends of the earth. This is the restoration of the kingdom to Israel. But it is not only to Israel. It is the restoration of the kingdom to all the nations as well. The restoration of the kingdom to Israel and the restoration of the whole world takes place at the same time!

Acts 1:6—"Will You at this time restore the kingdom to Israel?"

> ## *When He returns, He drives the devil and demons off the planet and brings about the first resurrection (Revelation 20).*

The first coming of Yeshua was not the time for the restoration of the kingdom to Israel. It was the time for the establishment of the international ecclesia. When He returns, it will be the time to restore the kingdom to Israel. That is the correct timing.

The righteous remnants of faith from every nation make up the international ecclesia. That ecclesia will be joined to Israel. The kingdom will be restored to Israel, and through Israel to the ecclesia, and through the ecclesia to all the nations. The kingdom is all one (Zechariah 14:9). Yeshua's Messianic kingdom on earth during the Millennium will have its capital in Jerusalem, but it will include and embrace all the nations.

At that time, there will also be a worldwide healing of planet earth. Nature will be restored when the kingdom is restored. Nature will be set free when sin and Satan are removed. The restoration of Israel includes the restoration of all the nations. The restoration of the nations includes the healing of all ecological problems.

Romans 8:21—"The creation itself will also be delivered from bondage to corruption into the freedom and the glory of the sons of God."

The glory of the sons of God is the power of the resurrection at the second coming. The fullness of Israel and the church bring the resurrection power of Yeshua, which sets free all of nature. The resurrection of human bodies and the restoration of nature are part of the same release of transforming power.

The restoration of nature in Romans 8 is connected to the restoration of Israel and the church in Romans 11. The renewal of nature takes place at the same time the government thrones of Israel are restored.

Matthew 19:28—"At the renewal of creation, when the Son of Man sits on His throne of Glory, you will also sit on twelve thrones to judge the tribes of Israel."

The word for renewal here in Greek is ***palig-genesia***, like a redoing of genesis. Renewal, regeneration, and restoration all go together.

Why do we always speak of "restoration?" Restoration means to fix or repair something that was in right condition once and now is broken. Why couldn't we just get it right the first time? The answer to that question, as many others, is that God is good, and we have sinned.

The word in Hebrew for "new" and "renew" is the same, **khadash, חדש**. It forms the root of the word for "month" which renews itself with each "new" moon. When we speak of "new heavens" and "new creation," it is actually a *renewal*. In the resurrection, we will receive "new" bodies, but they are essentially "renewed" or "transformed" bodies (I Corinthians 15:51).

When the Bible says to make new, it means to renew as it was in the original plan of God. **"Restore us O God to You and we will return. Make new [*khadesh* חדש] our days as they were of old" (Lamentations 5:21).** To make new is to renew; to make new is to restore. It is all part of the same overall biblical concept.

God made the world perfect. He gave us free will. We did much damage by our sin, so God's plan always needs to fix and repair damage. Each time God introduces something good, we tend to break it, so He has to fix it. The plan of God involves fixing, repairing, healing, and restoring.

Matthew 17:11–13—"Elijah will indeed come and restore all things. But I say to you that Elijah already came...Then His disciples realized that He was speaking about John the Baptist."

The message of the apostles and prophets always called for the restoration of all things; all things that were damaged since the fall of Adam and the sin of Satan. Elijah called for restoration in his generation. John the Baptist did in his. So, the prophetic message calling for the restoration of all things will return to God's people before the end of this age.

Elijah the prophet himself will not return, nor will Moses. They served the Lord faithfully in their generations and finished their jobs. However, God will raise up new men and women of God with anointings and callings analogous to Moses and Elijah to prepare the people of God in the end times (Luke 1:17; Malachi 4:5–6). No, they will not be the same as the prophets and apostles that gave us the Scriptures. That is not to be repeated. But apostles and prophets of the last days will be crucial in leading the people of God to our final victory.

Acts 3:19–21—"Repent therefore so that your sins may be wiped away in order that there might come days of refreshing from the presence of the Lord, and He will send Messiah Yeshua, who was appointed to you from times past, whom the heavens must receive until the time of the restoration of all things…"

The word in Hebrew for restoration is *tikkun* תיקון. It is found in the Hebrew version of this verse in Acts 3:21. The word *tikkun* is also found in the traditional Jewish prayer *aleinu* עלינו in which we pray for the "redemption of the world in the kingdom of El Shaddai."

The traditional Jewish prayer and the teaching of the apostle Peter have the same similar hope: a spiritual revival in this life will lead to restoring all the things wrong in this world. The restoration of the world takes place in the kingdom of El Shaddai.

The words "refreshing from the presence of the Lord" here in Acts 3:21 correspond to the "outpouring of the Spirit on all flesh" in Acts 2:17. Repentance comes first, then revival, then restoration.

We read about the hope of Romans 11:26 for revival in Israel. The revival in Israel is part of the worldwide revival of Acts 2:17; which is the same as the "times of refreshing" in Acts 3:21. The revival in Israel is connected with the world revival which leads to the "restoration of all things."

The visions of revival and of restoration are linked together. Repent, revive, and restore is the way of God's kingdom.

What do we mean by the restoration of all things? Let's look at the rest of the verse:

"…the restoration of all things, which God has spoken of from the beginning of time by the mouths of all His holy prophets" (Acts 3:21).

We are for every good thing described in the Bible from the beginning to the end. In the beginning the Garden of Eden was a perfect paradise. In the end, that perfect paradise will be restored and even better.

The restoration of the kingdom to Israel and the restoration of the whole world takes place at the same time!

Revelation 21:4–5—"He will wipe away every tear from their eyes, and there will be no more death, and sorrow and crying and pain will be no more...Behold I make all things new."

This is the restoration of all things. All things will be made new and whole and clean and beautiful, just as they were always intended to be. Paradise will be restored.

Everything that is good is to be restored. Was creation good? Yes. It will be restored. Was sin and death good? No. They will not be restored.

Was Solomon's kingdom good? Yes, except it was plagued with sin and didn't reach to all the nations. The kingdom will be restored to Israel, but much bigger and much better. It will include all the nations and be without sin.

Was the outpouring of the Spirit at Pentecost good? Yes. It will happen again and grow stronger and stronger until the **"glory of God fills all the earth" (Numbers 14:21; Isaiah 6:3; Habakkuk 2:14)**.

Let's summarize the teachings on restoration:

1. Matthew 17:11—The message of the prophets is to restore **all things**.
2. Acts 3:21—The restoration of all things happens at **Yeshua's return**.
3. Acts 1:6—The **kingdom of Israel** will be restored.
4. Romans 8:21—Restoration includes the **renewal of nature**.
5. Matthew 19:28—The restoration of nature happens at the **same time** as the restoration of the kingdom to Israel.
6. Romans 11:25—The full restoration of the ecclesia leads up to **revival in Israel**.
7. Romans 11:15—The restoration of Israel leads up to the **resurrection of the dead**.

What will the restoration of all things look like?

Imagine a world with no sin, no sickness, no Satan. Imagine the Garden of Eden restored and covering the whole world. Imagine a government and society of perfect peace and prosperity with Yeshua ruling as king over all the nations from Jerusalem. Imagine the heavens and the earth, God and man, restored to perfect harmony. That's God's plan.

The hope for the "restoration (*tikkun*) of all things" by the apostles in Acts 3:21 and the "redemption (*tikkun*) of the world in the kingdom of El Shaddai" in traditional Jewish prayer is what motivated us to call our spiritual family of congregations, ministries and friends: **Tikkun Global**.

Questions for Reflection

1. What is the meaning of the Greek word ***pleroma***?
2. What is the meaning of the Hebrew word ***Tikkun***?
3. How do the restoration of Israel and the restoration of the church affect one another?
4. Is restoration only spiritual or does it have natural dimensions as well? If so, what are they?

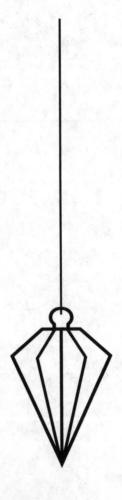

21

Turning the Hearts of the Fathers

One of the most important aspects of restoration is between parents and children, particularly between the father and the children. We could call this "Generational Transfer" or the "Generations Mandate." It has to do with right relationship between the older generation and the younger generation.

This is referred to in the prophecy about John the Baptist, quoting from the Book of Malachi, as "turning the hearts of the fathers." Let's look at both of these two prophecies.

> *There is no restoration of all things*
> *if there is not first the restoration between*
> *parents and children.*

Malachi 4:4–6—"Remember the Torah of Moses My servant... laws and judgments. Behold I send you Elijah the prophet before the coming of the great and terrible day of YHVH; and he will turn the hearts of the fathers to the children and the hearts of the children to their fathers, lest I come and strike the earth with a curse."

This is the last prophecy of the Old Covenant prophets. Remembering the Torah of Moses means to stand for absolute moral values in the face of a sinful generation. The reference to Elijah the prophet indicates the anointing to preach in the end times, not necessarily to Elijah as a person himself, but in the same power and spirit that Elijah had.

Notice that the prophecy of Malachi is similar to the prophecy of Joel and Peter, in that it refers to the time right before the second coming, the

> *The heart of a father is to create a safe home*
> *for his children and to take more joy in the*
> *children's success than in his own.*

"great and terrible day of YHVH." That is the third subject: end times events.

The fourth subject is parent-child reconciliation.

The prophecy of Joel/Peter also spoke of a great outpouring in the end times in which your "sons and daughters will prophesy" (Acts 2:17–18). The turning of the hearts of the fathers to the sons and daughters deals with healing and reconciliation within families.

That is an essential part of the prophecy about the end times. The revival over the whole world spoken of by Joel stands in opposition to the curse over the whole world spoken of by Malachi. We choose the blessing not the curse.

The darkness in the end times will be intense. There will be sexual perversion as in the days of Lot; violence and murder as in the time of Noah; anti-Semitism as in the time of Haman; a snake-worshiping government as in the time of Moses; and so on. All those are connected with this last evil: the breakdown between the generations.

I was listening recently to the words of a "rap" song in which an angry son was telling how he had been beaten by his dad as a child. The violence and anger were going in both directions. In the song, the dad was trying to ask the boy's forgiveness, but the boy didn't know if he could forgive or if it was even possible to fix the relationship between them.

This is a common experience for many. The generational breakdown is widespread. This is the curse spoken of by Malachi. All the other evils are connected to this one.

Spiritual transfer between parents and children is mentioned twice in the Ten Commandments. One is bad and one is good.

… visiting the sins of the parents upon the children.
—Deuteronomy 5:9

The influence of the parents' sinful behavior upon the children is obviously negative, while the benefits of the children honoring their parents are many:

> **Honor your father and your mother that your days might be long and in order that it might be well with you upon the earth.**
>
> **—Deuteronomy 5:16**

The negative spiritual transfer from parents to children is called a "curse." The positive spiritual transfer is a "blessing." According to Malachi the curse of negative relationships between parents and children will reach epidemic proportions worldwide in the end times.

The key for a fruitful and healthy life in the children's generation is learning to break the parental curses by forgiving them (and not repeating or overreacting to their mistakes); and then to receive the blessings by honoring them and listening to their advice.

The restoration process normally starts with the fathers, but it can come from the children. The heart has to be turned. Turning of the heart can mean "giving attention." It means listening, caring, and trying to understand.

The restoration between the generations is particularly important among us as a faith community. Failures and mistakes of the older members in the congregation can repel the younger generation. Sometimes the older generation does not see how their "zeal" can seem strange to their children. (I remember one of my sons mentioning that Isaac had likely been traumatized by the fact that his dad almost killed him.)

There is an essential role reversal or transition as the parents and children grow older. Physically the child reaches his peak strength at thirty; at age fifty to sixty the physical strength of the parent starts to slow down. Psychologically, the process takes longer. There is ability for a younger person to take more leadership as he becomes more mature, and the older parent figure must know how to release authority gradually.

There is a great attack on families and family values today. What would have been obvious a generation ago about family order is collapsing quickly. Since God is Father and Yeshua is Son, the family model is the universal and primary structure of relationships. Relationships between parents and children must be our top priority. Keeping our families healthy demands a huge amount of time, effort, and communication. Those relationships grow and develop as the children grow older and form their own nuclear families.

The father must transition from player to coach; from setting agenda to giving advice; from leadership to oversight. (I am constantly explaining to our younger team members how I am transitioning to more of an oversight role and expecting them to take more responsibility.) Transition process is gradual and takes a longer time than one would think. One should think in terms of a decade, not a month.

We distinguish between levels of leadership authority, somewhat based on age, or at least maturity:

1. Oversight

2. Leadership

3. Management.

Senior oversight should provide wisdom and perspective. The primary decision-making is on the number 2 level of "leadership." The leadership can function more quickly and confidently if there is senior oversight in place. The main work is done on the number 3 operational level of management.

In the ancient priesthood of Israel, the older Levites would release primary leadership at age fifty and then stay working as assistants to those who served as their helpers before that time (Numbers 8:25–26). The age may be older in our generation, but the principle holds true. Many leaders do not train others to replace themselves and do not stay on to serve them afterward.

An older person continues to grow in love and wisdom, even if his hands-on leadership ability slows down. He continues to grow in influence through releasing authority. The executive position decreases but the honor position continues to increase.

> ## *When the parent and children's generations are healed and restored, we will have a "people made ready for the Lord."*

The difference between oversight and executive leadership is what I call the "number 2" principle. Ideally it is the number 2 person in hierarchy who does the executive leading while the number 1 person in hierarchy does the oversight. It is difficult to oversee and lead at the same time.

This principle is based on the relationship between the Father and Yeshua. As we mentioned in chapter one, the Father is greater than Yeshua (John 14:28), yet the Father has delegated to Yeshua all authority (John 5:22–23, 26–27).

We see this example in Joshua leading the armies while Moses raises his hands on the mountain. Joseph rules the land under Pharaoh; Mordechai under Ahasuerus; Daniel under Nebuchadnezzar; etc. In Israel, the Prime Minister runs the government under the oversight of the President.

Senior leaders should maintain a position of honor while releasing operative authority. The elder in Scripture can mean a person on the leadership team of a local congregation, but it can also mean a revered senior leader in the wider community. This is called in Israel, "elder of the tribe." In the New Covenant, the apostles referred to themselves as "elders" in their latter years; not so much in the sense of local congregational leadership but as the respected figureheads of the community (II Timothy 4:6; I Peter 5:1; II John 1:1; III John 1:1).

(It seems to me that when a senior leader releases authority to a younger leader, the senior should stay on as a counseling-teaching-praying elder under the new leader, while still maintaining influence and oversight. Dan Juster has done that with me in the Tikkun Global board. I am transitioning to a similar role at the Revive Israel community, Tiferet Yeshua and Ahavat Yeshua congregations, and the Tikkun Jerusalem base.)

What goes up comes down. When honor goes up, blessing comes down. When giving goes up, provision comes down. When prayer and praise go up, power and glory come down.

We want to keep the cooperation between the generations. The older and the younger give an example of how to work together. It is not all young and not all old. The old and the new come together (Matthew 13:52).

Luke 1:17—"He will walk before Him in the spirit and power of Elijah; to turn the heart of the fathers to the children; and the rebellious to the wisdom of the righteous; to make a people ready for the Lord."

This prophecy came at the time of John's birth. Yeshua added that Elijah would "restore all things" (Matthew 17:11). The Elijah anointing will restore all things in the hearts of the people so that we will be "ready" for the return of the Lord.

The saints are to take John and Elijah's role in these end times. We are to make the people ready to restore all in Yeshua's kingdom. There is a two-stage "restore all" process. First, everything is restored within our hearts before the Lord returns. Then everything will be restored outwardly after His return.

1. Restoring all in the ecclesia happens right before the millennial kingdom.

2. Restoring all in the Nations happens afterwards, during the millennial kingdom.

Generational restoration is a key element in preparing our hearts. It is an essential mandate for the end times. Our God is a multi-generational God. He made covenant with Abraham and Isaac and Jacob. A godly attitude means we must have a multi-generational worldview.

We believe in covenantal relationships. I have given a little abbreviation in letters to summarize covenant principles: YS + OT = GT: Your Success (what is good for you); plus Our Togetherness (being and working together) leads to Generational Transfer. Our relationships must arrive at the end to a transfer to the next generation, or they will die out.

We should be desirous of the success of our friends' children and pray for them. Faithfulness to our friends' children and grandchildren is the last stage of covenant. It is the last stage of restoration and alignment.

Isaiah 59:21—"This is My covenant with them. My Spirit, which is

on you and My words which I have put in your mouth will not depart from your mouth, from your children's mouth, and the mouth of your children's children—from this time on and forever."

If God is my partner, He is loyal to my children. Therefore, I should be try to be loyal to my partners' children. When younger people like David Shishkoff, Ben Juster, Evan Santoro, Nathan Wilbur, Matt Rudolph, Troy Wallace, and many others, can see me as a spiritual dad or uncle, then I know we have fruit that will remain.

This prophecy is a two-way street. It is initiated by the "fathers", but it is followed up by the "children." The word here for children is *banim* בנים which is literally "sons" but can be translated as "sons or children." If the fathers' generation will turn their hearts to the sons' generation, then everything else can be healed. Malachi 4 promises that if the fathers' hearts will turn, so will the children's hearts turn in response.

The heart of a father is to create a safe home for his children and to take more joy in the children's success than in his own.

The children will have to overcome the flood of lies, anger and disrespect in the world today. A child of God is one who maintains an attitude of honor and respect. He steps out of that stream of the "rebellious" and the "stubborn." That demands a huge sacrifice of integrity, humility, obedience, and love on the part of the children's generation.

Malachi's prophecy is a vital and urgent word for our time. There is no restoration of all things if there is not first the restoration between parents and children. This is a banner statement for us in these end times, "turning the heart of the fathers to the children and the heart of the children to the fathers."

The God who said, "All Israel will be saved" and "I will pour out My spirit on all flesh," is the same God who said He would "turn the hearts of the fathers to the children and the hearts of the children to the fathers." Can we see the restoration of families and the reconciliation between parents and children as a central mandate from God in these end times? We have to; if not, the whole world will be cursed.

When the parent and children's generations are healed and restored, we will have a "people made ready for the Lord." That was the message of John the Baptist that introduced Yeshua in the first century. It must be our message as well in this century before Yeshua's return.

Questions for Reflection

1. What is the last prophecy of the Old Testament and why is it so important?

2. What are the positive and negative influences of parents upon children?

3. How is leadership transferred to the upcoming generation?

4. What is the "two-way street" relationship of older and younger generations?

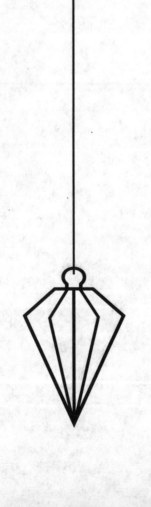

THE GLORIFICATION OF JERUSALEM

This is the __final alignment__: Jerusalem glorified. Earthly Jerusalem lines up with heavenly Jerusalem.

CHAPTER

22

The Future Glorification of Jerusalem

Alignment has order and direction. The order is so that we can cooperate; the direction is so that we can arrive at our goal. Ultimately the goal of the New Covenant and the earlier Israelite prophets is the same. The goal of both being reconciled into one is portrayed prophetically as the transfiguration of the city of Jerusalem into a glorified form.

In the New Covenant, the end times' vision is found primarily in the Book of Revelation. Its final two chapters (21–22) describe just that: a gloriously transformed New Jerusalem, which descends from heaven (Revelation 21:2).

> *The future glorification of the city of Jerusalem takes place during the Millennium as the capital of Messiah's kingdom on earth.*

The vision for the Israelite Messianic kingdom is found primarily in the prophet Isaiah. That vision reaches its climax in the last few chapters (60–66). Those chapters describe something quite similar: the city of Jerusalem restored and glorified (Isaiah 60:1; 62:1). This is the *final alignment*: Jerusalem glorified. Earthly Jerusalem lines up with heavenly Jerusalem.

To understand this final alignment, we have to compare the last chapters of Revelation with the last chapters of Isaiah. When these chapters come into harmony in our thoughts, we will better understand the idea of Zion glorified.

The comparison of heavenly Jerusalem in Revelation 21–22 and earthly Jerusalem in Isaiah 60–66 is similar to the comparison between the two views or pictures of the second coming found in Revelation 19 and in Zechariah 14.

Revelation 19 describes Yeshua coming down out of heaven, leading the warrior angels into a battle on the earth. Zechariah 14 describes the nations of the world attacking Jerusalem, and YHVH coming to fight them, with His feet finally standing on the Mount of Olives. Those two passages describe the same event but with two different perspectives.

Revelation shows the heavenly viewpoint; Zechariah shows the earthly viewpoint. One without the other does not make sense. What battle is Yeshua coming down from heaven in Revelation 19 to fight in? Who is this YHVH whose feet stand on the Mount of Olives in Zechariah 14?

The harmony of Revelation 19 and Zechariah 14 gives a clear line of understanding for the end times and the second coming. It also creates a definite line of alignment. The line goes from heaven to earth. The line goes from heavenly Jerusalem to earthly Jerusalem. It has a specific timing: when the armies of the nations of this world attack Jerusalem.

That definition of alignment makes us choose sides. We have to stand on one side or the other. Yeshua is coming to fight. He puts a "line in the sand," or in this case, a line from heaven to earth; He puts a line between Jerusalem and the nations. This is a line of confrontation.

We also mentioned how that same line of confrontation is described in **Psalm 2:6: "I have set My King on My holy mountain, Zion."** The powers of this world are seen in rebellion against God. This alignment is the pretext for the great war of the end times. God's alignment represents His authority on earth: His King, Jesus; His capital, Jerusalem.

The rebellion in this world is directed against the authority of God. God's authority is in His King and His King's capital city: Jesus and Jerusalem or, in Hebrew: Yeshua and Yerushalayim. God's line of authority is drawn between these two points. The link between Jesus and Jerusalem is the alignment of authority that the world wants to attack.

> *To understand this final alignment, we have to compare the last chapters of Revelation with the last chapters of Isaiah.*

The church has preserved the lordship of Yeshua; Israel has preserved Yerushalayim as the capital. As the church and Israel come into harmony, the link between Jesus and Jerusalem is restored. God's line of authority is reestablished, but so is the target of rebellion. This alignment also prepares the way for the harmony between heaven and earth. That final link is the joining of heavenly Jerusalem and earthly Jerusalem.

The ancient Israelite prophets provide the context for understanding the New Covenant apostles. The end of the Book of Isaiah provides the context for the end of the Book of Revelation.

Revelation 21–22 provides the heavenly viewpoint; Isaiah 60–66 provides the earthly viewpoint. You cannot understand one without the other. Where does the heavenly Jerusalem of Revelation 21 descend to? How does the Jerusalem of Isaiah 60 shine with the light of God? When you put the two together, it all begins to make sense.

As the connection between Revelation 19 and Zechariah 14 brings clarity to the second coming, so the connection between Revelation 21 and Isaiah 60 brings clarity to Paradise Restored. Revelation 21 describes the glory of heavenly Jerusalem; Isaiah 60 describes the glory of earthly Jerusalem. The merger of the two is the final restoration.

It is like a sandwich: if you have only one piece of bread, the sandwich falls apart; if you have both pieces of bread, you have something to hold on to. This is the final harmony alignment of the Bible: heavenly and earthly Jerusalem sandwiched together. It puts the Christian concept of heaven together with the Jewish concept of the kingdom.

The Book of Revelation was written by the Apostle John, approximately twenty to thirty years after the other writers of the New Covenant had finished their works. John, who was Yeshua's closest friend and most beloved disciple, had years to meditate and pray about what was written in all the rest of the Bible.

John summarizes and gives symmetry to the whole Bible. Genesis 1 and 2 describe creation and paradise. Revelation 21 and 22 describe the renewal of creation and paradise. Genesis 3 describes the victory of Satan; Revelation 20 describes the victory over Satan. John gives revelatory understanding of main themes of the Scriptures from beginning to end.

In those last two chapters of Revelation (21–22), we see the final destiny of many biblical themes from the Law and the Prophets, such as:

– Heaven and earth (21:1, 10)

– Jerusalem (21:2, 10)

– The Bride (21:2, 9; 22:17)

– Mosaic tabernacle (21:3)

– Reversing the curse (21:4; 22:3)

– Restoring all things (21:5)

– Divinity of Messiah (21:6; 22:13, 16)

– Punishment of the wicked (21:8; 22:15, 18–19)

– Glory of God (21:11, 23)

– Tribes of Israel (21:12)

– Gates/walls of the city (21:12–13; 21–22)

– Twelve apostles (21:14)

– Angels (21:17; 22:8–9)

– Breastplate of Aaron (21:19–20)

– Gentile nations (21:24)

– Rivers of Eden (22:1, 17)

– Throne of God (22:1, 3)

– Tree of Life (22:2, 14)

– Benediction of Aaron (22:4–5)

– Government (22:5)

– Scriptures (22:7, 9–10, 18–19)

– Sanctification (22:11)

> *Understanding the unity of Eden and Jerusalem allows us immediately to see the unity of the scriptural plan from beginning to end.*

- Reward of the righteous (22:12)
- David's seed (22:16).

The last chapters of Revelation are the final words of Scriptures. A variety of themes come together which may not have seemed united previously in the Bible. John "puts them together." He weaves them into one last tapestry. He puts the last pieces of the puzzle together so that a larger picture is seen.

When John speaks of a new heaven and earth, the rivers of life, the tree of life, and of God dwelling with mankind, he is referring to the restoration of Eden. This is paradise restored. This is more than paradise restored; this is paradise perfected. This is more than paradise perfected; this is paradise glorified. Genesis 2 speaks of Eden; Genesis 3 speaks of Eden lost. Revelation 21–22 speaks of Eden restored and glorified.

Natural creation will be restored and filled with glory. The rocks and the trees will be alive. Fruit will drip with eternal life, wisdom, and healing. A drink of water will fill you with joy. Animals and humans will be friends. Precious jewels, rainbow colors, and beautiful music will fill the Garden. The word **Eden** עדן means "delightful and delicate." All of creation will be full of delights. This is the glorification of natural creation.

This delight-filled restoration includes Jerusalem as well. Eden is restored; Jerusalem is restored. Eden is glorified; Jerusalem is glorified. The two great biblical themes of Eden and Jerusalem come together. They become one. Four times in this section are Eden and Jerusalem described as being one and the same:

Revelation 21:1–2—"I saw a new heaven and a new earth...I saw the holy city, heavenly Jerusalem, coming down from heaven..."

Revelation 22:2—"In the middle of the street of the city and on the

bank of the river on either side was the tree of life..."

Revelation 22:14—"...in order that they might have the right to the tree of life and to enter the city by its gates."

Revelation 22:19—"God will take away his portion from the tree of life and from the holy city..."

Read those verses again, please. There is one unavoidable conclusion. Eden is Jerusalem. Jerusalem is Eden.

The tree of life is on the bank of the river of Eden, which flows out of the center of the city of New Jerusalem. The righteous have the privilege to enter the city by its gates and to eat of the tree of life. The right to enter Jerusalem and to eat of the tree of life is the same. Eden and Jerusalem are one. (Garden of Eden in the midst of Jerusalem made me think of Central Park in New York or Merlion Park in Singapore: There is a park in the middle of the city.)

Eden and Jerusalem have always been one. This is revealed to us here in the last chapter of the Book of Revelation. That is a stunning and inspiring thought. The last chapters of the last Book of the Bible unveil the mystery that Jerusalem and Eden are the same.

This should have been obvious all along, but it is easier to see in retrospect from the Book of Revelation. Yeshua was crucified on the Tree in the same place where the sin on the tree was committed. Yeshua was raised from the earth where Adam was made from the earth. Yeshua's sacrifice and the sacrifices of Solomon's Temple and the sacrifice of Isaac are all in Jerusalem. They return to the place where it all started in order to solve the original sin.

The continents were separated in the generation of Peleg (Genesis 10:25; I Chronicles 1:19). The name *peleg* in Hebrew פלג means to "divide." If the continents are imagined to be joined back together (as presumably they will be in the regeneration), Jerusalem is found in the center. It's not difficult to see the continents fitting together by looking at a globe.

The rivers came out from Jerusalem. (Remember that water flows downhill, from the source to the end—two of the rivers end up eastward in Iraq, but the two others went out presumably southward and westward). Those rivers in the Millennium are found to flow from the center of Jerusalem,

| *The last chapter of the Bible combines the*
Christian idea of heaven with the Jewish hope
for Jerusalem and puts them both inside the
universal utopia of a perfect paradise. |

bubbling up from under the eastern door of the Temple (Ezekiel 47:1).

Where else would God have placed the capital of His kingdom? There is one plan of God from beginning to end. It started in Eden, which was always intended to be the center of God's kingdom, continued through the binding of Isaac, to the capital of David, to the crucifixion of Yeshua, to the first apostolic community, to the millennial kingdom, and ultimately to Eden restored.

This is the center of God's perfect world, the place where heaven and earth come together. Understanding the unity of Eden and Jerusalem allows us immediately to see the unity of the scriptural plan from beginning to end.

The name Jerusalem appears 814 times in the Bible; the name Zion, 153. That's 967 references. If we add Moriah, My Holy Mountain, Jebus, the Holy City, the city of the great King, etc., we could round off the number to an even one thousand times. What could be so important about this location that warrants one thousand references in the Scriptures?

The re-unification of Eden and Jerusalem proves that God had everything all planned out from the beginning, through the middle, and to the end. The end of the plan is the same as the beginning. The final contractor's building fits exactly the original architect's plans. The last chapter of the Bible combines the Christian idea of heaven with the Jewish hope for Jerusalem and puts them both inside the universal utopia of a perfect paradise.

Questions for Reflection

1. What are the two different perspectives in which the books of Isaiah and Revelation describe the glorification of Jerusalem?

2. How do "Jesus and Jerusalem" represent the two points of conflict described in Psalm 2?

3. What is described in the last two chapters of the Bible in the Book of Revelation 21–22?

4. Are Jerusalem and Eden the same place?

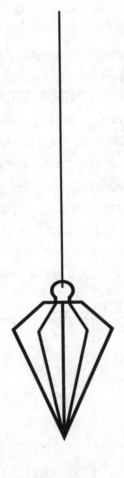

23

Present-Day Glorification of Jerusalem

At the very heart of the plan of God is the glorification of the city of Jerusalem. The glorification will take place in three general time periods:

1. Far Future
2. Future
3. Near Future.

> *Isaiah 60 is the key passage to understand God's plan for the glorification of Jerusalem in the present age.*

The *far future* glorification of the city of Jerusalem takes place in the new heavens and the new earth at the *end* of the thousand-year millennial kingdom. It is described in Revelation 21 and 22 as we studied in the previous chapter. That is the ultimate renewal and glorification of all things, with heaven and earth united, and paradise restored. Heavenly Jerusalem and earthly Jerusalem merge together.

The *future* glorification of the city of Jerusalem takes place *during* the Millennium as the capital of Messiah's kingdom on earth. This capital city and the kingdom are described in many passages of Scripture, too numerous to list here, of which the most detailed account is the final nine full chapters of the Book of Ezekiel.

After the revival and restoration of Ezekiel 36 comes the resurrection of Ezekiel 37, then apocalyptic war of Gog and Magog in chapters 38 and 39. Afterwards we find the description of the millennial kingdom in chapters 40 to 48, in extensive detail, concentrating on the city of Jerusalem.

> *The glory light happens simultaneously and in contrast to the darkness of evil in the world. Revival and persecution always go together.*

That millennial kingdom is also described briefly in Revelation 20. At the *end* of that millennium, Satan is released, and the city of Jerusalem is attacked once again. **"They went up onto the width of the land and surrounded the camp of the saints and the beloved city; fire came down from heaven from God and consumed them" (Revelation 20:9).** That means the city of Jerusalem will already have a certain glorified state or special position *during* the millennial period.

The attack against Jerusalem is not only the culmination of this age but also the age to come. That is the final rebellion at which point all evil is punished forever. During the millennium, there will still be many people who hate God. They will also hate Jerusalem. The devil will be released at the end to allow all the God-haters and Jerusalem-haters to attack the city and demonstrate their evil intentions.

The city of Jerusalem is called **"the beloved city."** Around the city is the **"encampment of the saints."** For all the thousand years, there will still be hatred and resentment against the holy city and the holy people. Jerusalem is the center gathering place of the people of God.

There will also be a glorification of the city of Jerusalem at this present time, in the very near future. This glorification takes place in this "pre-millennial" age and will reach its height during the tribulation period, right before the second coming.

> **Arise, Shine, for your light has come and the glory of YHVH will shine upon you. For behold darkness will cover the earth and deep fog the nations, but upon you YHVH will shine, and His glory will be seen upon you. And the nations will come to your light and kings to the brilliance of your shining.**
>
> **—Isaiah 60:1–3**

Isaiah 60 is a profound and significant prophecy for our time. It is quoted approximately a dozen times in the Book of Revelation! Isaiah 60 is the key passage to understand God's plan for the glorification of Jerusalem in the present age.

[Note: Since this prophecy is pre-New Covenant, there is an overlap, like all the ancient Israelite prophets, in envisioning the different future periods of the end time. This overlap of future prophecy has been described like seeing mountaintops on your way up to Jerusalem. As you come up the hill, you only see one mountain.

When you get to that mountain, you realize there was actually another one behind it. Then there is another mountain after that as well. So there is an overlap in the prophecies of Isaiah 60 to 66 about the time before the second coming, at the second coming, during the Millennium and at the New Creation. These prophecies have to be discerned and differentiated between those overlapping stages.

Since the prophecies of Isaiah 60 are referred to in the New Covenant as being fulfilled in all the different ages, we must understand that our viewpoint is only partial. We must be cautious not to overemphasize one part or another.]

The word for light, *oor* אור , appears three times in this verse. It takes us back to the Creation in which there was a type of metaphysical light created before the creation of the physical light of the Sun and stars (Genesis 1:1–3). It also points us toward the light of the promised Messiah (Isaiah 9:2), which was fulfilled in Yeshua (John 1:1–9).

The word for glory, *kavod* כבוד, appears numerous times throughout the surrounding passages. It reminds us of the promise that the "glory of YHVH will fill all the earth" (Isaiah 6:3).

The word for shining, *zarakh* זרח, is connected with the shining or rising of the sun in the morning and is also the root of the modern word for phosphorus.

Isaiah 60:2 states that this shining glory will actually be seen on the city. (The word for "you" here is feminine; thus, it is referring to the city and not to Yeshua.) Something will be seen on or above or in the city. The glory of God will be seen. Mike Bickle refers to this as the "manifest glory of God resting on a city."

Can we imagine the visible and tangible glory of God manifesting itself over an entire city? Over the people of an entire city? Over the city of Jerusalem? On the buildings, in the streets, over the conference centers, children, elderly, Jews, Arabs? What part of this is pre-millennial, millennial, or post-millennial? We don't know for sure.

In its most minimal "pre-millennial" form, we could see this prophecy as referring to the presence of God in the hearts of the believing Messianic Jews, Arab Christians, and international Christians, living in Jerusalem. By inference, it would also refer to Spirit-filled believers in every nation of the world. We all together are a spiritual Zion.

The prophecies about Zion are not just about a city, but about the community of faith in every nation. Zion is both Jerusalem and the ecclesia at the same time. Hopefully, the people in the world around us will be able to sense the beautiful presence of the Lord in our lives.

However, if we are to hope for all Israel to be saved (Romans 11:26) and for the spirit of grace and supplication to be poured out on the inhabitants of Jerusalem (Zechariah 12:10), we can at least pray for a major Pentecostal-type revival for Jerusalem in the end times, right *before* the coming of Yeshua in glory and power.

We are not interested in just imagining this, but in dedicating our lives to prepare the way for this to happen. **"Prepare the way of YHVH. Make straight the path for our God. Every valley will be raised and every mountain and high place made low....And the glory of YHVH will be revealed, and *all flesh will see it together*" (Isaiah 40:4–5).** Let's work together to push and pull and move out of the way everything that is hindering until this physical manifestation of the glory is seen by everyone in the flesh.

It is possible to see and feel the manifest glory of God. It hovered over the encampment of the Israelites every single day and night for forty years in the wilderness. It appeared on the tabernacle in the time of Moses, on the Temple at the time of Solomon, and of course on the disciples of Yeshua in Acts 2. They saw and felt the tongues of spiritual fire upon them.

This promise would be like the hovering of the glory cloud, not over the camp, but over the city. The city is supposed to be like that encampment (Revelation 20:9). It would be like a Pentecost experience for the whole city. We are not told how long it will last. Will it be a day, a week, ten days, a year, three and a half years?

In any case, it may be the single greatest manifestation of God's glory at any point in history. **"Everyone who remains in Jerusalem will be called holy....Then YHVH will create over the whole established place of Mount Zion and over her assemblies a cloud and smoke by day and shining flaming fire by night; for over all the glory will be a canopy"** (Isaiah 4:3, 5).

This passage in Isaiah 4 is similar to that of Isaiah 60 in which the glory of God will cover Jerusalem. Wouldn't it make sense for that to happen in the time leading up to the second coming? Yet, it is hard to fit in with the final war and partial destruction in Jerusalem. Perhaps revival and war come at the same time. A judicious conclusion would be that there is a partial before-the-millennium fulfillment, a greater fulfillment in the millennium, and an ultimate glorification afterward.

We can't engineer this to happen. On the other hand, there is no reason not to give ourselves in every way possible to do our part in fulfilling what is clearly the will of God. What will it take to have this happen?

For Zion's sake I will not be silent and for Jerusalem's sake, I will not be quiet until her righteousness goes forth as a shining light and her salvation as a burning torch. And the nations will see your righteousness and all the kings your glory.

—Isaiah 62:1–2

We must teach on the subject; humble ourselves; repent; act righteously; pray; work for unity and reconciliation. We must share the gospel;

disciple; build the congregations; proclaim this prophetic message; and call for the right alignment so that the international ecclesia and the Messianic remnant can be ready for this to happen.

There are several other challenging aspects to this prophecy. Notice the "darkness will cover the earth" in Isaiah 60:2. This seems to be pointing to the period of time known as "the tribulation" (Mark 13:24) or "Jacob's trouble" (Jeremiah 30:7). Because of the darkness covering the earth at the same time, this must be referring to a period before the second coming. The glory is shining amid darkness.

A light bulb lights up when the wires are connected to the electricity. This is where the alignment comes in. When the Messianic remnant and the international ecclesia are lined up together, the wires "touch" in a spiritual sense. Spiritual Zion is connected to Jerusalem City. One end of the wire is connected to the heavenly generator; the other wire is "grounded".

Isaiah 60:1–2 is a prophecy about the manifest glory of God resting on the city of Jerusalem during the tribulation. There is light in the darkness. We don't know exactly what that will mean. The glory of God will manifest itself again in this world in some tangible way. Part of this will be fulfilled before the second coming, as well as after.

All prophecies of the end times speak of great revival and harvest but also of a time of great difficulty and persecution. The glory light happens simultaneously and in contrast to the darkness of evil in the world. Revival and persecution always go together. Salvation comes at the time of tribulation. In the darkness we are told to "rise and shine."

Perhaps the glory light that Isaiah refers to is only the invisible presence of God's spirit in His people on earth. What will be visible will only be the horrible tribulation and persecution. To what extent this glory is visible or not visible is not our concern. We serve the kingdom of God. We believe there will be an outpouring on all flesh in the end times (Joel 2:28; Acts 2:17), an outpouring of grace and supplication on the inhabitants of Jerusalem (Zechariah 12:10), and that all Israel will be saved (Romans 11:26).

> *Zion as the city and Zion as the people of*
> *God will both come into a process of divine*
> *glory, both now and in the world to come.*

As part of these promises of revival, we believe in a glorious spiritual outpouring on all the saints in the midst of tribulation and deep darkness. The city of Jerusalem has a strategic place in this outpouring. Of course, this is the reason why my wife, Betty, and I live in downtown Jerusalem, and why our Tikkun Global base is located here.

The teaching that the ecclesia will be removed or raptured immediately before this period is extremely deceptive and damaging. First of all, that kind of thinking goes against all the teaching of Scriptures, which say that God strengthens us in the time of trouble, but does not remove us (John 15:18, 20, 25; 16:2, 20–22, 33; 17:15).

Secondly, our job is to make a people prepared for the Lord (Luke 1:17, 3:4–6). If we tell people they will not even be here, they will obviously not be prepared. In such case they will fall. I am concerned that pre-tribulation rapture teaching will leave people unprepared for the difficult times ahead and, thus, make them turn away from God in huge numbers.

In Yeshua's teaching about the seed and the soil, He said that there is a "shallow" soil that easily rejoices, but the moment difficult times come, they fall. **"Yet he has no root in himself but stands only for a short time. When tribulation or persecution comes because of the word, then he falls immediately" (Matthew 13:21).**

The rapture happens at the end of the tribulation, not at the beginning. It is part of the events connected with the second coming and the resurrection of the dead. There are seven clear references to the rapture in the New Covenant (Matthew 24 [two references], Mark 13, Luke 17, I Corinthians 15, I Thessalonians 4, II Thessalonians 2). Every single one of those seven has a clear time reference in it. Every single one says, "after the tribulation."

The glory of the Lord in the prophecies of Isaiah is accompanied by a strong response from the nations. One of those reactions is a supernatural outpouring of finances. **"The wealth of the nations will come" (Isaiah 60:5).** (This prophecy is repeated several times: Isaiah 60:9; 60:11; 60:16; Zechariah 14:14; Revelation 21:24–26). The word here for nation is *goy,* גּוֹי, which can be translated either as "Gentile," "nation" or "Gentile nations."

[The word *goy* has a double meaning, either positive or negative. In the negative, Gentile can mean "pagan, unbeliever, not part of the covenant." It can also mean simply "nation." When a Gentile receives the Lord, he becomes part of the covenant and is no longer a Gentile in the pagan sense of the word. He retains his national identity. The national identity of every person is strengthened when he becomes a follower of Yeshua, but all the pagan parts of his history are washed and redeemed.]

How is this prophecy of the coming of the wealth of the Gentile nations to be fulfilled? Is that to the church? Or to Israel? Or to the Messianic remnant? Or a partial fulfillment to all three. Its ultimate fulfillment is that the nations will bring tribute to King Yeshua, ruling from Jerusalem. As the nations brought tribute to King Solomon in his empire, how much more so will the nations bring their resources to bow down to Solomon's Greater Son, Yeshua.

Why should there be such an abundance of resources? Is there a partial fulfillment before the second coming? This could not be for greedy, selfish purposes or for a small vision. If the wealth is to come from all the nations, it must be a provision for a vision that will bless all the nations. I believe there is a promise here from God to provide the resources needed to share the gospel of the kingdom in every nation.

There is another rather extreme prophecy concerning the "nations"—it speaks of submission. **"Every nation or kingdom that will not serve you will perish, and those nations will be totally destroyed" (Isaiah 60:12).** Again this prophecy is likely to be fulfilled in three stages: before, during and after the Millennial kingdom. In whatever time or stage, the manifestation of the glory of God's kingdom always elicits a response of submission and worship.

The manifest glory of God, as described in Isaiah 60, will draw a supernatural response, both in financial supply and in submission to authority.

The attack of the nations against Israel by Gog and Magog is prompted by jealousy over the finances, the authority, and the glory (Psalm 2:3; Ezekiel 38:12, Revelation 20:9).

In the prophecies at the end of Isaiah about the glorification of Zion, there is another factor that is mentioned repeatedly. It is the response of the Gentile nations to come, to help, to build, to plant, to bring the children from far away, and in general to be partners with Israel in this glorious end times restoration (Isaiah 59:19; 60:2, 3, 5, 6, 7, 9, 10, 13, 14, 16; 61:4, 5, 9, etc.). There are too many references to list.

What a beautiful thought! Zion's glory brings the Gentile nations into cooperation with Israel for the restoration of the kingdom. They will want to serve and help. They will want to be part of every aspect, both the spiritual and the practical. This seems to be best understood as having some aspects before the Millennium kingdom and others during it.

This touches the heart of Yeshua: Jews and Gentiles in cooperation to serve the vision of Zion glorified. We will serve Yeshua's kingdom together and it will be glorious.

Finally, let us remember that the words for Jerusalem and Zion also have a universal and international spiritual meaning. Therefore, we should conclude that the glory manifest in Jerusalem would also be manifest in prayer meetings and congregations all over the world.

The glory of the Lord will be upon Zion. Followers of Yeshua around the world will be connected to that glory by faith. The same glory can appear anywhere. There will be a network of little "Jerusalems" in the spirit in every fellowship of Yeshua's disciples in every nation around the globe. They will be spiritually connected through love and faith.

Thus, the before-the-millennium spiritual blessing of Jerusalem will have both a local manifestation and a worldwide manifestation. The centralized nucleus and the worldwide network will reinforce and strengthen one another as the spiritual power of the Lord flows back and forth between them. They are "electrically" connected in the spirit.

Zion refers both to the city of Jerusalem and to the people of God in every location. Zion is to be glorified. If the city is not to be glorified, then neither will the "spiritual sons" of Zion. Either Zion is glorified or not, in both senses of the word. Zion as the city and Zion as the people of God will both come into a process of divine glory, both now and in the world to come. Let's let our light shine in the midst of the most horrible darkness around.

Questions for Reflection

1. Why would the nations attack Jerusalem at the end of the Millennium after Yeshua has already been reigning for a thousand years?

2. What is significant about the prophecy of Isaiah 60:1–3 in which the glory of Jerusalem shines in the "midst of darkness?"

3. What would it look like for the city of Jerusalem to be "glorified" during the tribulation time?

4. What is the response of the Gentile nations to the glorification of Jerusalem?

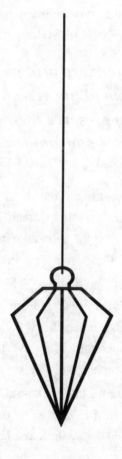

CHAPTER

24

The Glorified Bride

When we speak of the glorification of Jerusalem, it is more than a city or a garden. Essentially, it is people. A city is made up of the people who live there.

This group of people is also pictured as a Bride or as a Glorified Woman. This woman is both the city of Jerusalem and the community of saints around the world. **"Another great sign was seen in the heavens: a woman clothed with the sun, and the moon under her feet; and on her head was a crown with twelve stars" (Revelation 12:1).**

> *The plan of God is to bring all people into harmony and to fill them with divine glory, yet to let them preserve their own colorful personalities and ethnic diversities.*

The Bride, glorified Jerusalem, and the community of saints in the end times are all one. Notice that this woman is being attacked in a way which is definitely indicative of the tribulation period (verses 3–7). This is another example of the glorification of Zion in the present age.

It is the people who will be glorified. This has to do with a concept called "the glorification of the saints." This means that in the resurrection, the people of God will receive bodies that shine with light and glory power. This glorification is God's perfect will for every person. (I talked more on this topic in my book *The Apple of His Eye*.)

Abraham was told that his children would be like the stars of heaven (Genesis 15:5). Not only will the children be numerous like the stars, but they will have bodies that shine like the stars. Just as some stars have more

The Bride, glorified Jerusalem, and the community of saints in the end times are all one.

magnitude than others, some people will have more glory magnitude than others (I Corinthians 15:41). The glory is determined by how they served the Lord in this life.

Moses experienced a bit of that glory when it rubbed off on him as he spent eighty days and nights fasting in the presence of YHVH (Exodus 34:29). Paul went on to explain that the glory we will receive for eternity will be like Moses' but much greater in power, and it will be permanent, not temporary (II Corinthians 3:7–11).

This is also the meaning of the Aaronic blessing. The blessing is that YHVH would make His face to shine upon us (Numbers 6:25). The glory is in the soul of God. It is in the soul of Yeshua. That glory shows through the eyes. The eyes are physically located in the exact center of the head and face. When glory comes through the eyes, then the whole face shines. The glory of God passes to us from face-to-face intimacy, eye-to-eye contact, and soul-to-soul connection (II Corinthians 3:18). The meaning of the blessing of the High Priest is for you to experience intimacy with God and glorification in His presence.

When God promised to fill the earth with His glory (Numbers 14:21; Isaiah 6:3; Habakkuk 2:14, Psalm 72:19), He meant primarily through the people, not just the rocks and the trees.

One of the first people to prophesy about the glorification was Deborah in her victory song. **"Those who love Him will go out as the sun in its power" (Judges 5:31).** It is possible that Yeshua took His disciples to Mount Tabor where Deborah wrote this prophecy. The disciples asked Yeshua what the kingdom of God would be like. He said that within a few days He would show them. On top of the mountain, He was transfigured before their eyes, with His face, body and clothes shining with light (Matthew 17:2; Luke 9:29).

Yeshua gave an example of the glorification at the place where Deborah prophesied that it would happen. [It is possible that the mountain was

231

<u>not</u> Tabor but Hermon near Nahal Dan. In any case, the transfiguration on the Mount follows up the prophecy of Deborah.]

Daniel prophesied about the glorification and connected it to the resurrection. He also mentioned that the degree of glory would be connected to the degree of righteousness (Daniel 12:2–3). Paul further explained that the degree to which we will receive a glorious "vessel" after the resurrection has to do with what we chose to do with the earthen vessel we have in this life (II Timothy 2:20–21).

Paul explained that we each have a personal destiny, which is to be conformed to the image of Yeshua. There is a process of becoming Christ-like, which begins with being foreknown, then predestined, then called, and then justified. The last step of our destiny is to be glorified just as Yeshua is glorified (Romans 8:30).

The transformation to a glorified body will take place when our bodies are changed at the resurrection (Philippians 3:21). The body we have now is only earthen. Should we die and go to heaven before Yeshua's return, we would be in glory but only heavenly. After the resurrection, we will have a glorified body that can function both in heaven and on earth.

The degree of glory in the next life is connected to the degree we have suffered with the Lord in this life. Suffering in general does not produce glory. Suffering which comes from evil opposition, because we are walking with the Lord, does produce glory. You could make a mistake on one side or the other. You could suffer meaninglessly. Or you could miss out on the character development that comes through faithfulness during opposition. That is the testing of heart which prepares you for glory later on (I Peter 1:7).

The disciples taught that being partakers of the suffering of Christ makes you by the same degree a partaker of His glory. (See for example: Matthew 5:11–12; Luke 6:22–3; John 12:23; Acts 5:41; Romans 8:17; II Corinthians 4:17; Hebrews 2:10; I Peter 1:11; 4:13–14; 5:1.) Don't miss your opportunities for glory by being a "comfort-zone-only" believer.

Stephen, the first martyr, was the greatest example of glorification in the midst of suffering. His face was transfigured just when he was about to be stoned to death (Acts 6:15).

We are glorified not only as individuals but as a group. Our glorification as a group is what makes us a beautiful and glorious "bride." The Bride is the group glorified. Much has been taught on being the Bride, so I will only touch here on the aspects of its connection with Jerusalem and alignment.

Notice that the Bride is Jerusalem. **"Come, I will show you the bride, the wife of the Lamb...he showed me the holy city, Jerusalem, coming down from heaven from God and the glory of God was in her" (Revelation 21:10–11).** The Bride is Jerusalem, heavenly Jerusalem descending, with the glory of God. This verse is referring to some of the verses about the glorification of Jerusalem, which we read from Isaiah (Isaiah 60:1–3, 19; 61:10; and 62:3–4).

The Bride is the group of people living in heaven in a glorified form. They come down to meet the bridegroom. The Bride is the population of the city of heavenly Jerusalem. The wedding takes place at the joining of the heavenly city with the earthly city. This is the time to consummate the marriage and become one in spirit and body.

The Bride of Yeshua is the group of people who have been sanctified, glorified, and dedicated their lives to intimacy with Him. It is a group of beautiful people. Their glorification is a unified glorification because of their love for Yeshua. The unity is part of being the Bride.

One of the characteristics of this group of people is their total identification with Jerusalem. They love Yeshua not only as a husband but as a king. He is the king of Jerusalem. The heart of the Bride and the destiny of the city of Jerusalem become one. The Bride is thrilled at her husband's beauty, glory, authority, and victory. She loves Him for who He is. He is the head of the church—she is the church (Ephesians 5). He is the king of Israel—she is Israel. He is the ruler of the nations from His capital in Jerusalem—she is Jerusalem. The identity of the Bride is glued to the identity of Jerusalem.

The glory light inside the city comes from God, from Yeshua, and from us. There is no need of the sun. The Bible does not say that there will be no sun, but that the light of the glory will overshadow the sun. The sun and stars will still exist. This is confirmed both by John's vision and Isaiah's (Revelation 21:23; Isaiah 24:23; 60:19).

We spoke in section two about the family of Abraham. As the sign of the Abrahamic covenant family is circumcision, the sign of the glorified family is the rainbow (Genesis 9:13). God made a covenant with Noah for all the nations of the earth (Genesis 9:9). The covenant with Noah came first. The covenant of Abraham came afterward in order to help bring the Noahic covenant to pass by blessing the Gentiles (Genesis 12:3).

The plan for all the nations came beforehand. That was the original intent: to do something glorious with all the nations of the world. The rainbow is the sign of that first purpose. The different colors represent the different ethnic groups. The shining light represents the saints glowing with the glory of God. The light of the rainbow is a refraction of the light of the Sun. The glory of the saints comes as a reflection of the glory of God in the face of the Son.

Yeshua and Peter taught that the end times would be like the times of Noah (Luke 17:26–27, II Peter 3:5–8). Here's a fascinating thought: the rainbow emerged after the flood. First comes the flood; then comes the rainbow. In the end times, there will be a flood of evil, a flood of judgment, but also a flood of revival. Out of that flood period will emerge the glory of God's people all over the world. Together they will look like a glorious rainbow.

The plan of God is to bring all people into harmony and to fill them with divine glory, yet to let them preserve their own colorful personalities and ethnic diversities.

The great wedding happens when heaven and earth are joined together. Heavenly Jerusalem joins with earthly Jerusalem. There is a harmony of the two locations and the two identities. Heavenly Jerusalem has been identified with the church, earthly Jerusalem with Israel. The Bride has to harmonize both those identities within her.

Therefore, the Bride must have this double yet harmonized identity. A light cooperation between Israel and the church is not enough. There must be a movement in heart of the international "Gentile" ecclesia to be

| *The glory of the saints comes as a reflection* |
| *of the glory of God in the face of the Son.* |

joined with Israel. There must also be a movement in heart of the Messianic remnant that fully embraces and adopts the international church.

The ecclesia and the remnant must become one in heart. This is where the alignment takes place: in the unity and partnership between the international ecclesia and the Israel remnant. There are two different yet profound mysteries taking place at the same time.

[There is no contradiction between our heavenly identity and our earthly one. What is it that makes up our "ethnos" identity? **Revelation 7:9** describes the multitude coming from every **"nation, tribe, people and tongue."** I see here four different components of human identity.

1. We are citizens of a **nation**: we vote, pay taxes, fulfill civic duties, have legal standing.

2. We are born of tribal, parental **lineage**: that is our physical DNA with a line of descendants.

3. We are part of people's **culture**: a person can choose to learn and identify with the history, food, music, festivals, lifestyle, and life cycle of any people group.

4. We speak a **language**: language is a key element defining people groups; it includes literature, education, and way of thinking.

Those different elements comprise our "color." It gives us human variety and diversity within the universal spiritual family of God.]

My friend Ariel Blumenthal points out that in the mystery of **Ephesians 3:6** the Gentiles would be **"partners in the inheritance, partners in the body and partners of the promises."** These three partnerships are described by the three Greek words, all starting with the prefix *"syn, sum"* from which we get English words like *synchronization, synthesis, and sympathy.*

1. *Synkleroma*—**"co-heirs."** This legal term suggests a total equality of shared privilege, like two brothers who have bound themselves

together, *dependent on each other* for whatever inheritance and success they can expect to receive from their common father.

2. *Synsoma*—"co-body" people, "of one body." In the gospel, Jew and Gentile have become one living organism, with the same spiritual blood of Christ and the same heavenly DNA. Whatever happens to one part of the body affects the whole.

3. *Summetocha*—"co-promise" people, or "partakers of the same promise" in Christ Jesus. "Promise" is in the singular, not "promises." In keeping with the rest of Paul's writings, specifically referring to the pre-figured, gospel promise made to Abraham, as taught in Romans 4, 8:17, and Galatians 3:26–29.

This mystery is about the multi-racial relationships within the community of faith. There is a second mystery about the relationship between the community of faith and our Messiah savior. The first is like a family; the second is like a marriage.

That second mystery, found in **Ephesians 5:27, 32** is the marriage of the church to Christ. **"So that He may present her to Himself a glorious church with no spot or blemish. This is a great mystery, but I speak of Christ and the church."**

The mystery marriage of Christ and the church in Ephesians 5 is parallel to the mystery partnership of Jew and Gentile in Ephesians 3. The Ephesians 3 Jew-Gentile partnership is a necessary pre-requisite to the Ephesians 5 marriage. This is a "double mystery." This is the parallel mystery: Christ and the church marriage along with Jew and Gentile partnership.

One might ask: "If this were so, is there a dual nature within the Bride? Does she have a split personality?" One way to see an answer is to look at Queen Esther. I can think of no biblical figure that more represents the glorified Bride than Esther. She was beautiful, gracious, royal, pure, magnificent. Did she have a "dual identity"? Of course. She was both Persian and Jewish. In Esther we see the perfect reconciliation of the double identity of the Bride as Israel and the church.

We can see another example of the dual identity in the physical body of any bride. She has two eyes and two thighs and two breasts. Part of the beauty of the Bride is that very dual nature. The dual nature must be in perfect harmony. It is like a dance—not a dance between two people, but a dance between two groups.

It is the dance of the double camp.

> **Return, return O perfect one. Return; return that we may gaze on you. What would you see in the Shulamite? She is like the dance of the double camp. How beautiful are your footsteps in sandals, O prince's daughter...**
>
> **—Song of Songs 6:13; 7:4**

The Bride of Messiah is a group of people. It is actually two groups of people coming into perfect harmony, like two camps dancing together. The harmony of Jew and Gentile is part of the beauty of the Bride in Yeshua's eyes. He enjoys watching the poetry of the dance of the double camp. It is not schizophrenic; it is harmonious, balanced, and beautiful.

The name *Shulamite,* שׁוּלַמִּית, is a personal name, but it is also the feminine form of "perfect one."

In Hebrew, the suffix "ayim" means "double." Shulamite's eyes and thighs and breasts are all described with this double suffix. The word for double camp is *makhanayim,* מַחֲנַיִם, also has that double suffix. It is an encampment that is doubled. Here the double camp is dancing. It is a symphony of two choirs.

The dance of the double camp is the graceful ballet movements of the Bride of Christ. It is the global alignment we have been talking about. It is the beauty of the Bride. And this dance of the double camp has a gracious and miraculous synergy to it.

Questions for Reflection

1. What does the "glorification of the saints" mean?
2. What is the connection between the Bride of Christ and the city of Jerusalem?
3. What is the meaning of the "rainbow"?
4. How is Queen Esther an image of the Bride of Christ?
5. What is the "dance of the double camp" of the Shulamite?

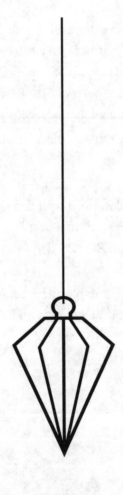

5

SYNERGY

Synergy means that teamwork will produce an overall better result than if each person within the group were working toward the same goal individually.

25

Synergy and Synthesis

Alignment leads to synergy.

Much of this book has talked about cooperative relationships within the worldwide community of faith. We described it as a symphony and as a synchronizing. The Greek prefix "syn" is like the Latin prefix "com." It means "together with."

> *Working as a team allows for God to move in a way that is beyond any one of the leaders and even more than each one together. The "team" becomes its own identity with its own synergy.*

First, we have sympathy or compassion. This is love, which allows us to feel what others feel. That leads us secondly to cooperation, synchronization, symphony, or alignment. But there is another stage, a third stage. The joining together leads to a result that is greater than the parts.

"The whole is greater than the sum of the parts." This is called synergy. Synergy can be defined as: the interaction between two or more organizations or agents to produce a combined effect greater than the sum of their separate efforts.

Ezekiel Synergy

Notice the synergy of Ezekiel the prophet in chapter 37. In the first half of the chapter, we see the miracle of the resurrection of the dead. That resurrection happens in two stages. Ezekiel has to prophesy twice, in two stages: first to the dry bones and then to the wind (or spirit). When he prophesies to the bones, they begin to come together, to be joined and to take on flesh (Ezekiel 37:6).

Then he is told to prophecy to the wind. As he does, the spirit comes to give life to the dead (verses 9–10). There is alignment and there is synergy. The power to align pulls them together. The power of synergy brings resurrection. The unity of the body is the alignment; the resurrection life is the synergy.

Then in the second half of the chapter, we see again that Ezekiel takes two pieces of wood and joins them in his hands. He joins the kingdoms of Judah and Israel (Ezekiel 37:16–18). After they become one, something else happens. First there is the unity, then the kingdom. The uniting of the two sticks results in restoration of the Messianic kingdom (verses 22–26).

Like Ezekiel, we have to pray to bring together, unify and heal the community of faith and the kingdom of God (Luke 11:17). The pattern remains the same: alignment leads to synergy.

Teamwork Leadership

Synergy means that teamwork will produce an overall better result than if each person within the group were working toward the same goal individually.

It is like the biblical principle that one can chase a thousand, and two can chase ten thousand (Leviticus 26:8; Deuteronomy 32:30).

If a sign is to point out a direction, it must be in some kind of triangular or arrow shape. An arrowhead points to the direction. An arrowhead has a lead point and then two side points. I like the idea of leaders working in teams of at least three. Those three can then rotate in their leadership according to their different gifting and spheres of authority.

Dan Juster, Eitan Shishkoff and I have had that kind of relationship. Dan is more teaching oriented, Eitan more pastoral, and I tend to the prophetic. Eitan and I were submitted to Dan in the United States. Dan and I submit to Eitan in matters of the Galilee and our Israeli fellowship. They submit to me in our global vision coming out of Jerusalem.

That rotating leadership and submission allows for different qualities and viewpoints to come out. There is leadership, teamwork, and submission. We should seek to work with others who are happy to both submit and lead. (As we said earlier, leadership always involves mutual submission.)

When the three of us work together, something else happens. It is more than just the addition of Dan, plus Eitan, plus Asher. There is a synergy

> *When the people come together in*
> *cooperation and co-partnership,*
> *God's power will be revealed.*

that is more. The whole is greater than the sum of the parts. An additional "three-fold cord" dynamic takes place (Ecclesiastes 4:12). We try to encourage this kind of three-fold cooperation in all leadership teams.

This synergy can also happen with five. The "five-fold" ministry of apostles, prophets, evangelists, pastors, and teachers (Ephesians 4:11) were meant to work together. Their gifts complement one another. The five together should not be just the five, but their teamwork produces something else. The "team" itself has a value and beauty to it. It is more than just "pulpit rotation."

Our senior oversight team at Tikkun usually operated with five. Paul Wilbur, Michael Brown, David Rudolph and Don Finto have been part of that "five-fold" pattern at different times. We seek to develop teamwork leadership in every congregation, in every project, and in every ministry. Teamwork leadership creates synergy.

We always seek to work in partnership and cooperation. I had a blessed cooperation with Eddie Santoro at Ahavat Yeshua, before he went to be with the Lord, and today with Jonathan Moore and Yonas Belay. At Revive Israel our team included Youval Yanay and Tal Robin, and the Tikkun Jerusalem base Ariel Blumenthal and Jeremiah Smilovici. At Tiferet Yeshua in Tel Aviv, I worked for years with my friends Ari Sorkoram, Ron Cantor, Gil Afriat and Moti Cohen.

In our global family vision, David Demian and I have a sweet relationship of submitting one to another. The chemistry of that relationship in itself comprises the message. It speaks louder than words.

Working as a team allows for God to move in a way that is beyond any one of the leaders and even more than each one together. The "team" becomes its own identity with its own synergy.

Ecclesia Synergy

Synergy can be likened to a forest and trees. In the Garden of Eden, there were many trees. Yet when all were put together, it was more than just a group of trees. It became something more; it became paradise. Some people "don't see the forest for the trees." The forest itself is more than just all the trees together. When they are together, a picture of a wide and beautiful landscape emerges that is beyond just the trees.

We studied above about the mystery of **Ephesians 3:6**—that the Gentiles would be **"partners in the inheritance, partners in the body and partners of the promises."** This is the alignment. The alignment of the ecclesia is a mystery because it will become something that no one has ever seen. It is not just 1 plus 1 equals 2, but rather the 1 plus 1 produces another thing altogether, a number 3. That third thing is unknown.

Whatever it is, it will not only be a surprise, but it will be exponentially powerful. What will this mystery ecclesia/Remnant alignment be? What will it do? How powerful is it?

> **To enlighten the eyes of everyone to know what is the fellowship of the mystery which from the beginning of the ages has been hidden in God who created all things through Jesus Christ; so that now the multiplied wisdom of God might be made known through the ecclesia to the rulers and authorities in the heavenly places.**
>
> **—Ephesians 3:9–10**

Ephesians 3:10 here is such a profound verse. The eternal, manifold and manifest wisdom of God will be displayed through a certain group of people. That group of people is the ecclesia. When the people come together in cooperation and co-partnership, God's power will be revealed. As we become one, the manifest wisdom of God will be made known through us. That's a lot more than you and I putting our meager portions of wisdom together.

The ecclesia synergy will produce something that will be awesome enough to stun and replace the systems of authority in the world today. The political governments of this world will be replaced by a new spiritual hierarchy of love and glory. (The word in Greek for "rulers" in this verse is *"arche"* as in the word "hierarchy.")

| *Our spiritual critical mass will produce an explosion of grace and beauty.* |

It will be a wonderful divine family in both heaven and earth **("the whole family in heaven and earth"—verse 15)**.

It will be filled with God's nature and demonstrate all of who God is and what He can do **("be filled with all the fullness of God"—verse 19)**.

It will reflect the glory of God **("glory in the ecclesia"—verse 21)**.

This synergy will produce something beyond all imagination, which is stronger than all evil powers. It will become the authority of God on the earth; it will be the family of God the Father; and it will be filled with all the wisdom, glory, and fullness of God.

I suppose that's pretty good. And I suppose it is worth it for us to keep working through all these alignment and reconciliation challenges, so that the synergy will be released to reveal this awesome craftsmanship of God. David Demian says, "We are building a critical mass." Our spiritual critical mass will produce an explosion of grace and beauty.

Synthesis

A similar idea to synergy is synthesis. Synthesis is the third step in a process: thesis, antithesis, and synthesis. It means that first there is an idea. As this idea develops, there is another idea that seems to be the opposite, or at least contrasting. There is tension between the thesis idea and the antithesis idea. Then the two are reconciled into a third idea. That is the synthesis, where the two ideas come together to produce a third idea, which is better than the other two.

We could compare this to paradigm shifts between Peter and Paul. Peter was essentially a Galilean. His worldview in the kingdom of God was all of Israel. He led the revival in the first half of the Book of Acts. Peter led the follow-up stage to Yeshua Himself. That is quite an honor and accomplishment.

In the second half of the Book of Acts, we find Paul leading the kingdom strategy. He was the "follow-up" to Peter. Peter had a definite revelation that Gentiles could be saved (Acts 10:32). However, he did not have a revelation of God's full plan for the Gentile church (what we are calling here the international ecclesia).

The plan of the ecclesia was given to Paul. Paul in a certain sense was the "antithesis" to Peter's "thesis." Peter totally affirmed that Paul's view was correct, although he admitted that it was a little difficult for him to grasp it fully (Acts 15:6–12; II Peter 3:15–16).

While Peter's view was more Galilean, Paul's view was more "Jerusalemite." [We have the wrong impression about Paul because he was born in Tarsus (Turkey). However, he grew up and was educated by rabbis in Jerusalem (Acts 22:3). His worldview was not Turkish but Judean. He saw the kingdom extending from Jerusalem to the ends of the earth, just as the Judean prophets did before him (Isaiah 2:2–5, 49:6; Micah 4:1–3; Acts 1:8).]

We have come now to a stage in history where Israel and the Israelite remnant are being restored. Does this mean that we are returning to the worldview of Peter? Or do we maintain the worldview of Paul? It seems to me the answer is: neither.

Peter was the thesis; Paul was the antithesis. We are looking for the synthesis in these end times. We are looking not only for the combination of the two, but a third worldview that will produce something even better. In some ways, the writings of John are a synthesis of Peter and Paul since he wrote after they had gone to be with the Lord.

The writings of John have special meaning for us as we look to a synthesis of Peter and Paul. John wrote about the unity of heaven and earth, and of the consistency of the biblical plan from beginning to end. That is our goal, to serve the total plan of God in a wholistic and comprehensive way.

God's Thoughts

God had His own thoughts before He created the world. He had a plan. That plan is known to Him alone. He is revealing it to us in stages. All the plan is found in Messiah Yeshua and comes through Him. The entire mysterious plan is manifest in the process of synthesis and synergy combining the international ecclesia and the kingdom of Israel.

> *The entire mysterious plan is manifest in the process of synthesis and synergy combining the international ecclesia and the kingdom of Israel.*

Everything starts with the <u>thoughts</u> of God.

When He has a thought and we don't know it, it is a <u>mystery</u>.

When he transfers one of those unknown thoughts to us, it is a <u>revelation</u>.

When we understand God's revelations to us, it becomes <u>wisdom</u>.

God does not have many revelations or mysteries, only thoughts, because He already knows everything. However, God has purposely given us a degree of free will so that we can surprise Him a bit. The only surprises or mysteries to God have to do with our actions and reactions.

For instance, God was surprised at how evil we could be in the abominations of child sacrifice (Jeremiah 32:35); He was surprised at how people could act in faith beyond any expectations—like the centurion in Luke 7:9 and the woman with the issue of blood in Mark 5:30.

(Our ability to surprise God is only limited. It is like a father who has a little child who prepares a birthday card for him. He is not really surprised because he saw it coming; and yet there is a wonder in receiving what the child wanted to give.)

God built into the system a way in which we could surprise Him with the mysteries of our own hearts. Let's try to surprise Him with something good; something that will make His heart glad. I imagine that the synergy in our lives through Yeshua will produce something so beautiful and glorious that it will be a surprise blessing to the heart of God, even though He already foresaw it.

It will be like Adam seeing Eve for the first time in the Garden of Eden. It will be like Noah looking up and seeing that shining and colorful rainbow on the first day after the deluge. Or like Ezekiel seeing the dry bones resurrected. Or like John seeing heavenly Jerusalem coming down in all her glory. Let's dedicate our lives to make God's heart happy.

Questions for Reflection

1. What is the meaning of the expression "the whole is greater than the sum of the parts"?
2. What is the meaning of the expression "thesis, antithesis, synthesis"?
3. Was the worldview of the apostle Paul from Tarsus or Jerusalem?
4. Can we surprise God?

2040 and the Jerusalem Syndrome

We are often asked if we know what the date of the second coming is. The answer is unequivocal: **No**. We don't know and no one knows (Acts 1:7). I would like to mention a number of interesting circumstances that are likely to occur around the year 2040.

The Jewish calendar is based on a letter system. Aleph **א** equals 1; Tav **ת** equals four hundred. The year 2040 on the Jewish calendar is "Tav-Tav." In other words, the letters come to an end. There are some Jewish mystics that have already claimed that year to be the end of the world.

There will undoubtedly be a flood of false Messianic claims and extremist cults exploding in every stream of Judaism all over Israel around that time. Yeshua specifically warned about "false messiahs" in the end times (Matthew 24:5, 11, 24).

In addition, the late Ayatollah Khomeini said in 2015 that Israel would be destroyed in twenty-five years. Radical Shiites in Iran took this as a literal prophecy and have begun celebrating the annihilation of Israel in 2040. Each year on the holy day of Al Quds (remembrance of the holy city, Jerusalem), they parade in the streets of Tehran looking forward to that date. I recently saw an article in the Israeli press about the parade. It showed a picture of nice-looking, young Iranian girls with full Islamic robes carrying little model rockets and missiles, calling for the destruction of Israel in 2040.

Through Iran's influence on Shiite Muslim fanatics all over the world, their 2040 annihilation dream may well spread to other groups.

Traditional Rabbinic calculation considers AD 2023 to be 5,784 years since creation. While that figure seems to be less than the recorded biblical account, it adds another perspective to the question. In that counting, there are over two hundred years to go before the end of the symbolic sixth millennium and the start of the seventh, sabbatical millennium. (Obviously, there is not a perfect calculation of days or years to the end times, yet we do want to note the pattern of the times and seasons.)

Revelation 9:14–18 states that in the final period before Yeshua's return there will be a massive world war in which one third of the world's population will be killed. (That would be approximately three billion people!) The army described in Revelation 9 of two hundred million soldiers is said to cross over the Euphrates River.

Let's not forget that in 2033 the Christian world will celebrate two thousand years from the crucifixion and resurrection of Jesus, and the Pentecostal outpouring in the same year. In biblical prophecy and modern eschatological literature, there is an expectation of a seven-year period of end times' prophecies to be fulfilled before the second coming. The year 2033 plus seven equals 2040 as well.

I imagine that there will be plenty of Catholics, Protestants, Pentecostals, Charismatics, traditional Jews, and Messianic Jews coming up with wild, end-time scenarios at the same time. Yeshua warned not only about false messiahs in the end times, but also specifically about **deception** (Matthew 24:4, 5, 11, 23, 24 and 26). Even the "elect" can be deceived (verse 24). We must be extremely "sober" when it comes to interpreting end times events.

Demographic studies show that world population should cross 9 billion in 2040. We can only imagine the type of crises there will be in such issues as global warming, food resources, disease epidemics, economic collapse, water, air pollution, and so on.

Things are likely to get "crazier" every day. Thank God, we know from Scriptures that after these difficult times, there is a much better world coming.

Let's end with just a warning about Jerusalem Syndrome. "JS" is a known medical disease, a psychotic disorder, in which people come to Jerusalem and start to believe they are some kind of biblical figure that has come back from the dead. There are lots of Elijahs, John the Baptists, and Jesus' running around here.

There was recently an unfortunate video going around on Israeli social media showing a young American, Christian man walking around the Galilee pretending to be Elijah the prophet, calling for fire to come out of the sky to burn up the Israeli policemen who had come to arrest him. Well, instead of fire from the sky, they zapped him with a taser shock gun to subdue him.

This is a demonic spirit of deception. When we begin to deal with prophecies about the end times, there is a tendency to get unbalanced. Not everyone has to be hospitalized for psychosis. This is a general spiritual atmosphere that affects everyone—including me and including you. It is like lust or pride or worry—it is just there. Let's be careful not to be affected by the spirit of deception.

The tendency of this spirit is to cause self-aggrandizement. It might make you just a tiny bit inflated as to how important you see your own spiritual experiences and revelations. You think you know more than anyone else. You think you have a special prophetic anointing and authority that no one else has. Fight against spiritual pride. Pride always leads to deception.

All spiritual revelation carries the temptation to pride. **"Knowledge puffs up" (I Corinthians 8:1).**

During the years of being criticized by some conservative evangelical brothers and sisters in Israel, I tried my best to humble myself and listen. I don't want to be deceived any more than anyone else does. We charismatics get very excited about the word of God, and sometimes that excitement ends up in exaggeration. But exaggeration is wrong.

I am trying to learn to speak more circumspectly yet maintain a fervent spirit about the purposes of God. As we walk in the knowledge of Scriptures and power of the Holy Spirit, let us remember to stay humble and honest. Let's honor and love those around us as better than ourselves (Romans 12:3, 10; I Corinthians 13:1–3; Philippians 2:3).

With all the supernatural and apocalyptic things going on around us, it is imperative for us to remain correctable, sane, balanced, and walking in integrity.

Appendix

Over the past couple of decades, there has been a lot of controversy about the functions of apostles and prophets; and even about the use of those terms. Now there is a new trend, which I see as positive: to use family-type language, such as spiritual fathers, mothers, brothers and sisters. This family language is becoming more popular in the global community of faith.

However, because of such controversy concerning the Ephesians 4:11–16 gift ministry roles, I thought it would be good to include here as an appendix a statement, hopefully clarifying the issues and bringing balance to this complex topic. This statement was composed by a cooperative effort of several of us together to address some of the more prominent issues:

Need for Integrity and Humility in Charismatic, Apostolic, and Prophetic Ministry

Those of us who believe in the legitimacy of apostolic and prophetic ministry today, confirm the need for accepted ethics of integrity and accountability. We stand against certain aberrations promoted by some charismatic leaders and some who identify themselves as apostles and prophets.

This statement is fueled by genuine love for the different members in the body of Messiah and is meant to be a call for repentance, righteousness, humility, honesty, purity, integrity, accountability and correctability among all of us who believe in the supernatural work of the Holy Spirit.

Let us remember that Jesus (Yeshua) is the Chief Priest and Apostle of our faith (Hebrews 3:1). Since He is Lord of all, any ministry should reflect an attitude of service and submission. Prophecy should always be motivated by love (I Corinthians 13:2) and be given with the awareness that we only know in part (I Corinthians 13:9). Therefore, the way we express ourselves should be void of any arrogance and self-promotion.

We believe in the five leadership gifts from Ephesians 4:11 ff. — apostles, prophets, evangelists, pastors and teachers. It is sometimes beneficial to identify people who are functioning in these gifts so they can be released to fulfill their callings for the benefit of all. (Discernment is always necessary. Just as there are real apostles and prophets, there are also false apostles and prophets [Revelation 2:2, Matthew 24:11]).

Naming these functions should never be for the purpose of elevating the status of any individual, but only to clarify his or her service within the Body. When all understand their gifts and functions, they can work together in harmony to advance the kingdom of God more effectively. Leaders should never find their self-worth or identity from ministry labels or titles.

The functions of apostles and prophets are described briefly in Ephesians 4:11–16 and chronicled throughout the Book of Acts. Today in different cultures and streams of the ecclesia, these gift ministries find their expressions in different ways. Teachings about the roles of apostles and prophets in the body today are widespread, yet quite diverse.

All ministry leaders should be held to standards required of elders as outlined in I Timothy 3. They are normally affirmed and installed in these roles by a team of elder-level leaders, and walk in mutual submission with them. Apostolic and prophetic ministry are normative functions in the New Covenant ecclesia, along with evangelists, pastors, teachers, elders and deacons.

Individual charismatic gifts, including prophecy, are also to be seen as normative for New Covenant believers and not as elevating the person to a prideful, mystical level of importance over others (Numbers 11:27; Acts 2:17–19; I Corinthians 12:4, 11; 14:1, 24, 31, 39).

Affirmations

We affirm that:

1. Apostles and prophets have always operated in the church.
2. The restoration of the use of the terms *apostle* and *prophet* is not to establish a movement to replace other church streams, but to clarify

these scripturally based ministries.

3. New Covenant leadership is not measured by titles, but according to the fruit produced and by godly influence in peoples' lives. Apostles in the Book of Acts were recognized as such by the congregations that followed them.

4. Apostolic leadership should not seek to assert authority over others who do not see themselves as called to their sphere or stream (I Corinthians 9:2; II Corinthians 10:13).

5. An apostle may have an oversight role, but oversight is ideally exercised among a plurality of leaders who are mutually accountable.

6. Part of the calling of apostles and prophets is to seek unity and cooperation with all church streams that are true to the gospel (John 17:21).

7. Charismatic leaders today should understand and affirm the basic biblical doctrines that have always unified true believing Christians. All teaching should be tested by the authority of the Scriptures.

Mistakes

We recognize the following mistakes:

1. **Lack of Humility:**
   The functions of apostle and prophet require genuine humility and a desire to lift up others. We repent of arrogant statements that have come from some who have perpetuated these aberrations.

2. **Dishonoring of Historic Church Streams:**
   We reject any presentation of the restoration of apostles and prophets that would delegitimize the historic church streams, suggesting that they were not truly an authentic part of the full ecclesia.

3. **Claim to Authoritative Influence Like the Canonical Apostles and Prophets:**
   There is a great difference between the canonical apostles and prophets, and those who serve as apostles and prophets within the Body since their time. Modern-day apostles are not equal to the twelve apostles of the Lamb (Revelation 21:14).

4. **The Royal Apostle/Pastor Model:**

   We repudiate the model that elevates the role of apostle or pastor to a type of dictator or king where unilateral decisions are made without accountability. The biblical model of leadership includes teamwork and mutual submission.

5. **Non-Accountable Apostle/Prophet/Pastor:**

   We reject the claim that ministry leaders are not accountable to other leaders; and that only God can remove an apostle/prophet from their position (perhaps by the leader's death), even in the case of gross moral failure. We reject the use of "touch not God's anointed," to suggest that leaders are *only* accountable to God, as this often leads to abuse.

6. **Unaccountable Prophecy:**

   Prophecies in the church today are to be tested by mature elder-level leaders. Those who prophesy in a way that is proven to be inaccurate, need to repent and submit to a team of senior ministers for reevaluation.

7. **Imbalanced Prosperity Teaching:**

   We reject the misuse of the Bible's teaching on prosperity that places manipulative emphasis on giving to the one who is preaching as the primary way to receive blessing and enrichment. We believe that God meets our needs and provides abundance, so that we can bless others, not to accumulate material wealth for ourselves (Luke 12:15).

8. **Ignoring Biblical Character Standards:**

   We reject the idea that apostles and prophets are beyond the standards of character required for all elders, as taught in 1 Timothy 3 and Titus 1. The higher the level of leadership, the greater the demand for character (James 3:1).

9. **Undue and Unbiblical Authority:**

   Leaders should never pressure people to obey their instructions beyond the dictates of the individual's own conscience and of the Scriptures; nor use their leadership position as a means of demanding obedience to them.

Thanks

Special thanks to all who contributed to the writing of this book, or the events described here. They are of course too many to name. A few worth mentioning are:

Dan Juster, David Demian, Eitan Shishkoff, Paul Wilbur, David Rudolph, Don Finto, Ron Cantor, Michael Brown, Youval Yanay, Ariel Blumenthal, Lou Engle, Mike Bickle, Jane Hansen Hoyt, Bassem Adranly, Tal Robin, Ben Juster, Bill and Holly Wallace, Felipe Hasegawa, Sarah Gerloff, and above all, my beloved wife and life-partner Betty.

Thanks to all of you, and the many, many of you not named here, who have walked through this process of aligning ourselves with one another and with the Lord's purposes.